GARDEN
AND OTHER COUNTRY BUMPS

The authors' success with *1066 and All That*
amply qualified them to compile the History of
British Agriculture (post-Saxon) which they
left out of that book. They cover the whole
subject of Gardening (including Golf, but
omitting chestnuts), Country Life and Scouting.
The Great Open spaces (faces, etc.) are laid
bare by their spades, and nothing further is
left to be said (or written) about them. The
delicate question of Earth Control is handled
in a manner which, though frank, makes for
perfectly hygienic reading; but when they come
to Bee-keeping the authors are quite unveiled.
Everyone who loves (or hates) a garden will
wallow in the rich loam of their wisdom.

by the Same Authors
in Magnum Books and
Methuen Paperbacks

1066 AND ALL THAT

AND NOW ALL THIS

HORSE NONSENSE

CHUG

GARDEN RUBBISH
AND OTHER COUNTRY BUMPS

by

W. C. SELLAR

and

R. J. YEATMAN

*With affrontispiece and
numerous insulting illustrations by*
STEPHEN DOWLING
(Licentiate of the Royal Raspberry Society)

MAGNUM BOOKS
Methuen Paperbacks Ltd

A Magnum Book

GARDEN RUBBISH

ISBN 0 417 02050 3

First published 1936 by Methuen & Co. Ltd
Magnum edition published 1977

Magnum Books are published
by Methuen Paperbacks Ltd
11 New Fetter Lane, London EC4P 4EE

Made and Printed in Great Britain
by Hazell Watson & Viney Ltd
Aylesbury, Bucks

CONTENTS

AUTHORS' NOTE

Several portions of this book have appeared
in *Punch* and are reprinted here by courtesy
of the Proprietors of that paper.

INTRODUCTION TO THE FOREWORDS

By the Authors

HAVING decided to write this rather deciduous little book, we thought it might be rather a horticultural idea to graft on to it some Forewords by certain exceptionally green-fingered friends of ours, namely *Dean Nuisance* (author of 100 and 1 Blameless Books for Garden Lovers), *Mr. Knatchbull Twee* (author of most of the others), *Angus MacFungus* (our old Scotch gardener) and young *Broccoli Bill* (assistant to the last named).

From our consultations with the first three of these we gathered that all Gardening Books amount to more or less the same thing : viz. " The Love of Nature, enshrined in page and parable " (Dean Nuisance) ; " Lovely Thoughts about *real* Lovelies " (Mr. Knatchbull Twee) ; " Mph ! " (Angus MacFungus). And young Broccoli Bill is unable, at present, to read (being no scholard).

We therefore decided that it would be unnecessary and, for certain rather bulbous reasons, inadvisable to invite any of them to actually read the manuscript.

. . .

*   *   *

FOREWORD

BY DEAN NUISANCE, HON. L.L.D., F. SUCC. SOC., ETC.

(Author of *Bloom and Blossom*, *T'wards the Garden Beautiful*, *Lovesome Things*, *Tomorrow in my Flowerpots*, *The Golden Hoe*, *The Marauding Grub*, *Earth's Benison*, *A Hundred and One Don'ts for Nature Lovers*, etc., etc., etc.)

The Trials and Tribulations of a Life Devoted (first) to My Flock and (second only) to My Flowers, vouchsafe (alas) but all too scanty leisure to peruse such compilations as this to which I now append (gladly, albeit hastily) my modest ' *Ite, bene factum'st !* '

Who doubts but that another volume added to the rich harvest of the quill which Our English Gardens have inspired should be reckoned all for joy ?

Indeed it is my Earnest Hope that the seed which these authors have sown may fall not upon Barren Ground. For in Gardening, as indeed in Life Itself, there is haply no Royal Road to Perfectness ; yet in the dark and chillsome eventides when golden hoe and pruning-hook recline in idleness enforced, can we not find in Books such Wisdom as, when cuckoo and when willow-wren return, will recompense a hundred-fold (and more) our studious squanderings of midnight oil ?

But hark ! 'tis the turn o' the year. Young April smiling through her tears, comes tripping——

AUTHORS : *Please. Dean, this is your Foreword, not your hundred-and-second book.*

DEAN : And now 'tis May-time and the marauding grub——

AUTHORS : *And now 'tis time Mr. Knatchbull Twee had a look in.*

*   *   *

FOREWORD

By Mr. Knatchbull Twee

(Author of *My Tiny Acre, What the Poppy told the Primula, Cottage Pie*, etc., etc.)

I'm sure your book is a *lovely book*, because all garden books are definitely *delicious*. Of course I haven't read it, but if one is a real Garden-Lover it isn't really *necessary* to definitely *read* garden books—just fondling the *covers* is *thrilling*.

Authors : *Thanks awfully, Knatchbull,—it really is too sweet of you.*

* * *

FOREWORD

By Angus MacFungus

our old Scotch Gardener

Yon's a' havers, ye pesty gowks

AND BY

Broccoli Bill

assistant to the above

Moy vayvourit vlowers is turmuts.

* * *

And finally :

A FEW BACKWORDS

contributed without invitation by

CAPT. W. D. PONTOON, M.C., R.E., RETD.

(Author of *A Realist's Garden*, *My Garden is a Loathsome Thing*
and other works intended apparently for Garden Haters)

*who somehow got wind of the fact that we were
writing a Garden Book.*

You Garden writers go on in a way that simply wouldn't
be allowed if you were writing about anything else : in
fact Nature is the only thing an author can be as futile
about as he likes and get away with it just the same. I
have little doubt that you have taken full advantage of
this extraordinary state of affairs.

Most books about the Country consist of three parts
Exquisite Fatuity and four parts Nauseous Erudition,
and are inexplicably blighted in all parts with 'albeits',
'alas's', 'peradventures' and other forms of literary
mildew. I have little hope that yours will prove an
exception.

My own books on these subjects are of course quite
different. . . .

*   *   *

FIRST BUMP

NATURE STUDIES

I. Brown Study (for Prefects only)

A SORT OF BIOGRAPHY
OF
DAME NATURE

I. RUDE BEGINNING

NATURE began with the Golden Age, when our rude forefathers (see rude illustration, page 2) used to *worship* Nature.

This was for some reason known as *Nature worship* and it was all (alas) rather vulgar and unsuitable and for Adults Only, since *fauns* and *centaurs* used to rush about playing fast-and-loose, hide-and-squeak and other not very Olympic games with the golden wood-nymphs and Bright Young Dryads of the period, while *satyrs* (hairy bounders) pranced brazenly up and down in a state of nature lewdly singing ' Cuckoo ! ' and other reprehensible slogans.

Indeed it is impossible to disguise the fact that Nature, in this rudist age, was rather a Bad Thing.

II. ROMAN PREOCCUPATIONS
Naturam expellas furca tamen usque recurrit.
JULIUS CÆSAR (?).

The Romans, who came after the Golden Age, also started off rather badly by worshipping Nature but

'A BAD THING'

soon abandoned this and invented the much more Roman idea of *pushing Nature out with a fork.*

They found, however, that whenever they did that, Nature (alas) invariably came back again. After a time they began to feel that it was a monotonous invention and not very triumphant after all, and were trying to think of a really good way of subjugating Nature when they learnt to their horror that they had pushed her too far and that Nature, recurring as usual in hexameters, but this time *with revengeful foot,* had saddled them with the most ineradicable and boring THING that has ever appeared on the surface of the Earth.

This Thing (they learned to their horror) was called the Cornucopia, and appeared to be a form of twisted symbolical bedsock, or umbilical jelly-bag, the true purpose of which, as they realized at the first glance, would never (alas) be revealed to mankind.

However, being by temperament a jollicose and bellicund kind of people, they faced up to the Thing and began defiantly filling it with Plenty of fruit and cereals and so on and tried not to lose their tempers when the fruit, etc., kept falling out symbolically at the top ; while the Greeks, whom they called in as usual to explain the tragedy, decided that the Thing was (on the one hand) an Eleusinian Mystery, since nobody was able to discover *what was at the bottom of it*.

Note.—Professor de Carot's conjecture (on the other hand) is not only undignified but groundless, not to say fruitless—see Fig. i.

The Romans never managed to conquer the Cornucopia, though they evidently succeeded at least once in pushing it out (probably with a fork) since it is recorded that they were furious when one of their leaders, *Fabius Cunctator, by delaying* (literally) *restored the Thing*. To this day Civilization continues to be helpless (with anger—or sometimes with laughter) in face of the Cornucopia.

Fig. 1.
Prof. de Carot's conjecture.

III.   TAME NATURE

The Romans were still coping with the Cornucopia when the Barbarians burst in on them, and Nature took advantage of the resulting confusion to become once more quite unsubjugated and disorderly, so that during the Dark Ages there was some danger of every-body going Cuckoo again.

It must have been about this time that the woods became full of filmy faeries, over-painted rouge dragons and badly behaved ogres.   Which was all rather Wizard

"C. of E."

but not really a Good Thing, so that Nature soon had to be converted to Christianity by St. Francis and St. Jerome and other zoophilous parsons, while good King Arthur and his jolly decent Knights cleaned up the mediæval backwoods and turned them into virgin forests, so that they would be ready for Queen Elizabeth.

As a result Nature became C. of E. and therefore
rather tame and, during the Age of Piety, more or less
fell into disuse except for bringing forth the fruits of
the earth in due season (i.e. just in time for the harvest
festival).

IV. BLAME NATURE

But with the coming of the Elizabethans, including
Shakespeare and Spenser and other unbridled poets,
Nature became much too jolly *again*, and gratuitously
introduced a *wave of Euphonious Shepherds* who went
tootling and footling about blowing their oaten pipes,
sowing their wild flutes, toots, etc., all over the place ;
so that everyone began dancing hey-hey and aroundelay
—those who were neat and whimsy succeeding, naturally, in footling it featly here and there, while those who
were just fat and clumsy merely succeeded (alackaday)
in tripping over the greensward.

Questioned a little later by the Puritans as to who-
the-devil all these Shepherds really were, Nature replied
(rather cryptically) that they were *Arcadians* and
threatened England with the Cornucopia. (Note.—
This gesture resulted, as usual, in the fruit, etc., falling

out symbolically at the top, whereupon a clever young wood-carver called Grinling Gibbons nipped in and got away with the Swag.)

Meanwhile the Puritans continued to adopt a rather high-hat attitude and insisted that Nature was not only a bad thing but practically a Scarlet Woman, while the poets made rather dashing experiments with Nature, such as holding (as t'were) the mirror up to it —though most people at this time were in favour of leaving it alone (as t'was).

V. DAME NATURE

Obviously things could not go on like this and even the wicked Wits of the Restoration Drama agreed that since the idea was now to do away with confusions of all kinds and have an Age of Reason, Nature would have to be tidied up like everything else. So in their cattish way they declared that she was a country frumpkin and vastly *passée*, and dubbed her *Dame Nature*.

In the following century Dr. Johnson showed his approval of this by arranging his friends tidily in a circle, with himself exactly in the middle, and walking about circumspectly in formal gardens making obleeging remarks about Nature, all of which began with

" Sir ! " In fact people were all behaving quite tidily
and reasonably until towards the end of the century
the Courtiers of France suddenly unhinged everybody,
including Dame Nature, by introducing a wave of

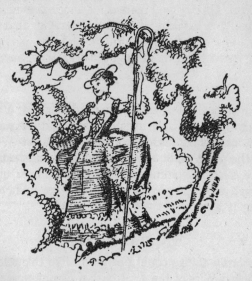

fancy-dress milkmaids and maddening *quilted-satin
shepherdesses* (with white wigs and white crooks tied
with blue bows) in a desperate attempt (apparently) to
dodge the French Revolution.

VI.   NATURE RUNS AMOK

Nature thereupon went mad, and in this condition
(alas) presented herself to *the greatest minds of the 19th
century* in such a bewildering succession of theatrical
disguises that *they also became unhinged*. Thus we find
the good Mr. Ruskin deliberately appalling himself

with an Alp (viewed from afar), Sir Walter Scott and other romantics declaring that Nature was not a bad woman but a Wild Thing, and the gentle poet Alfred (Lord Tennyson) seeing her Red (in tooth and claw); while Prof. Huxley and his friends shocked everybody, including the Archbishops, by declaring that Man himself, despite all his attempts to bring Nature to reason, was nothing more than a Natural Phenomenon.

VII. DAME NATURE, R.I.P.

This was too much, and from that moment all practical men set about the business, which to-day seems almost complete, of *abolishing Nature altogether*—not, however, without first allowing Ralph W. Emerson and

other frantic, romantic, not to say gigantic bores to embalm her memory in thousands of meaningless, contradictory and obviously balmy Pronouncements; while nowadays the surviving Nature-worshippers are (temporarily) permitted to establish Bird-Sanctuaries, Natural History Museums and Societies for the Fossilization of Rural England, in order to confirm the impression that Nature (the green bits you see through the windscreen-wiper) is an old has-bean.

But Nature is not quite done for yet, and revenges herself to-day by producing the fruits of the earth in season and out of season in such embarrassing profusion that at times the world resembles a gigantic Cornucopia the meaning of which will never (alas) be revealed to mankind.

This presumably is the reason why the great Nations of the Earth are now engaged in dressing themselves up like Ogres and preparing to destroy each other utterly by deluges of artificial earthquakes, pestilences and volcanoes in a desperate attempt (apparently) to dodge the millennium. . . .

II. GREEN STUDY FOR GUIDERS, MOTHERS AND OTHERS

NATURE IN THE RAW

(A Brief Survey of the Facts of Life)

" There is a lesson to be learnt from even the humblest of Earth's creatures. Do not think that you can escape it."
DEAN NUISANCE (Author of 101 *Don'ts for Nature Lovers,* etc.).

*" There comes a morning when we sense the teeming life
of the Earth astir with the Promise of Another Spring. . . .*

*From a myriad coppices hard-by the nesting song of the
weazel assails our nostrils. . . .*

*Down underneath a thousand sofas a thousand old
Scotch terriers are beginning to scratch again : they also,
we guess, are teeming with life. . . .*

*While far away in the orchards we hear the sap rising
in hundreds of old Scotch gardeners. . . .*

*As twilight falls two million cats bound quietly out via
the kitchen window and don't come back again for several
days. . . ."*

Whenever he comes across a teeming paragraph astir
with a myriad promises, coppices, etc., the reader
realizes (with sinking sap) that he is in for a dose of
Nature-Study : he knows that he is going to be told
(alas) the *Facts of Life.*

With difficulty he restrains himself from bounding
quietly out of the Country and not coming back for
several years. . . .

SPARE THE POD

" We determined to approach sex bravely, and frequently."
THURBER AND WHITE (*Is Sex Necessary ?*)

In the Victorian Age, when the Facts of Life were not
at all generally known, Nature was studied, elegantly
enough, for its own sake ; and a sorry spectacle (see
Fig. ii) was the Victorian gentleman who could not vie
with the Vicar in reciting the Latin names of his plants,
discourse upon the dust-bags of the dandelion and
bandy stamens and anthers with the squire over a
glass of sherry white-wine.

Fig. ii. A Sorry Spectacle.

All that is changed now. The purpose of Nature-Study to-day is much more serious : it is nothing less than to *reveal the Facts of Life to children and their parents, before it is too late.*

"Our object," says Dean Nuisance, "is to save the next generation from the ravages of sex—and to save it early, and if possible, entirely, *before the poison has gone too deep.*"

In furtherance of this object we now propose to reveal boldly and unflinchingly a few of the more amazing Facts of Life.

The Facts

" Almost immediately the two halves of the cell begin experiencing a desire to unite again—usually with a half of some other cell."
Thurber and White (Ibid.).

1. *The Secret of Life is Growth.* Thus if we have a little puppy or a little kitten and don't forget to feed it, it grows and grows and soon the puppy has become a dog and the kitten a cat—*never the other way round.* It is Nature's Law.

Growth goes in cycles, which are instructive. One of these is called the Cocoon cycle. If we have a little chrysalis and don't forget to waken it in the morning, it turns into a cocoon. Cocoons turn into caddices and caddices turn into lettuces ; lettuces in their turn, turn into coconuts. *Hence the milk in the pyramids.*

2. *The Secret of Growth is Protoplasm.* Protoplasm is a jelly-like substance, colourless and somewhat

Fig. iii.

featureless. It is not Dean Nuisance. But, like him, if it dries up it will die. (See Fig. iii.)

3. *The Secret of Protoplasm is oxygen, nitrogen, sanatogen, etc.* In fact it is just a question of thisogen and thatogen. *Note :* When teaching very young children

the secret of Protoplasm, nervous mothers will find it helpful to begin with the *feet*, explaining how each little tootsy has grown from its own little toetoeplasm ; from this it is easy to pass to, say, a photograph of a baby brother or sister and explain how this has grown out of its own little photoplasm, and a tin of cocoa from a grain of cocoplasm, and fountain-pens from little blots of onotoplasm, and so on. . . .

In addition to the above there are, naturally, a number of minor facts which a child will want to learn gradually as it grows older and begins *asking questions*. (The questions which children in their third year usually ask, are :

(i) What is pollen for ?

(ii) Who cares about father, anyway ?

(iii) Will I have whiskers when I grow up, like Aunt Margaret ?)

It is essential, for instance, that when this time comes the little one should have no illusions about the fact that *the pollen-grains from the anthers on the pistil of one florescence are translated by the insect to the sticky end of the stigma of the other florescence and thence send out long thin rootlets down the central cavity of the style which enter the matured ovules and later create the seed-lobes or cotyledons.*

Backward children cannot follow this easily ; yet it is clearly vital that your little girl should not become confused and imagine that the cotyledon sends down long thin cutlets into the dirty end of the pistol, or that one of Henry VIII's wives was called Anne Pollen, or that there are panthers at the bottom of her garden. The moment is critical—*one false step, and the poison is in* ; the little mind is wrecked, and when the time comes for her to leave Roedean and face the hustil and bustil of the world, *anything may happen*—she may ' come out ' in spots and never get presented at Court, or fall in love going down an escalator and marry (alas) beneath her station. . . .

There are many other facts we could tell you about Life. We could tell you, for instance, how the Plants protect themselves by Prickles and Poison-stings : but these are among the things that parents and little ones should learn for themselves. . . .

SPOILS OF CHILDHOOD

But theoretical study is not enough. Practical Field-work is essential. And as Dean Nuisance (alas, so rightly and ungrudgingly) observes : " What a wealth of health-giving activities has Nature of her bounty stored up for English boys and girls in our beloved pleasaunces and green meadows."

So here are some health-giving, practical hints which we of our bounty have thought it helpful to store up for the guidance of you English parents :

(i) Children with strong lungs and loud voices are apt to be noisy in the home (yes, they are, really) and will benefit by having their trumpets taken away and being set to blow birds' eggs, stag-beetles, snails, etc., inside out.

(ii) Overgrown toddlers are sometimes too heavy-handed for this work and these can safely be encouraged to increase their stamina by pressing flowers, twigs, eggs and possibly slugs, into nature albums and family Bibles, which can then be put away tidily in a drawer for the benefit of posterity.

(iii) Families with an Army tradition will run naturally to entomological field-work which keeps the youngsters busy catching butterflies and moths, and gassing them and sticking pins through their bodies. (We understand these studies are now compulsory in all German and Italian kindergartens).

(iv) Making old Country Wines and amateur cordials is a pastime in which the children can join ; the easiest, (dandelion-port, slug-gin, and the sweetish liqueur which our grandmothers used to distil from crushed-up moss and maggots) are not really very palatable but when daintily bottled will come in usefully for jumble-sales, raffles and the like.

SOME PRETTY EXPERIMENTS

Besides popping the fuchsias, and digging up the roots of prize dahlias to see if they are all right, all root, etc., enterprising children naturally pick up for themselves such fascinating tricks as growing grass from seeds out of the back of a little terra cotta pig in the nursery, or growing mustard-and-cress on father's damp flannel trousers in the coal-hole. But here are a few less-known experiments which can also be recommended :

A. *Bean-Watching*. Take a haricot bean and dip it in a little warm water. Now put it on some moist earth in a pot and watch the bean closely.

The bean will take a long time to grow—perhaps (alas) a hundred years—who knows?

If it does grow, it is very curious to watch the rootlet —who cares?

B. *Alternative Experiment.* Take a haricot bean and slip it into Nurse's stocking. Add a few stinging

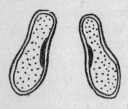

nettles and leave the stocking where you found it. She may want to wear it to-morrow— who knows?

If Nurse puts on the stocking, it is very curious to watch her face—who cares?

Section of French Bean (or possibly Dean Nuisance's bedroom slippers).

C. *What Every Toad Knows.* *How to tell a mushroom from a toadstool.* There are two ways:

(i) Get a toad and see if it sits on it. If it does, it was a toodstool.

(ii) See what it looks like on toast (the mushroom, not the toad). If it looks like toalstoods on toast, it was probably a toolstoad (or possibly a toast-stool).

EXPERIMENTS NOT RECOMMENDED

A. *Grrr . . . de Lion.*

Take a dandelion to pieces and look at the milk.

Now take an African lion to pieces and look at the little hairs on its chest: do not touch these, because when the lion is tickled *it pricks you.*

B. *Alternative experiment.*

Take a dandelion to pieces and try to look at the *corolla*. . . .

Now take a mountain-lion to pieces and try not to look like a gorilla. . . .

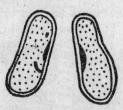

Dean Watching Bean.

SECOND BUMP

GARDEN RUBBISH

Caution! This Section is probably an Almanac

A SEARCHING LOVE-TEST FOR LUKEWARM
GARDEN-LOVERS : IN TEN SPITS [1]

Scene : The Garden Plot

*Characters who barge into the Plot, in the order we
wish they'd disappear :*

Dean Nuisance (Greenfingus Ecclesiasticus),
wordy perennial, of pendulus habit,
author of innumerable books relating
to the Garden Beautiful.

Mr. Knatchbull Twee (Narcissus Stylosus
Irritans), delicate hybrid (Ord :
violaceæ) of bogus habit, grafted
with difficulty on to common or garden
humanity.

Angus MacFungus ("Our old Scotch
Gardener"). An inexterminable
Pest.

Broccoli Bill. Assistant to above.

Capt. W. D. Pontoon, M.C., R.E., retd.
(Mighty like a Cactus!).

[1] In case you don't know, a *Spit* is a Spade Measure, meaning
*as much earth as a Gardener can dig without having to stop and spit
on his hands.*

21

SPIT THE FIRST

THE RULE OF TWEE

" The richest loam is valueless where Love guides not the spade."
DEAN NUISANCE (author of *T'wards the Garden Beautiful*, etc.).
" Whenever my eye lights upon the wee loveliness of the year's first snowdrop I literally scream with excitement."
MR. KNATCHBULL TWEE (author of *My Tiny Acre, What the Poppy told the Primula*, etc.).

DO *you* ? We mean (see Mr. Twee above) whenever your teeny-weeny eye lights upon the loveliness of the year's first something-or-other ?

You're not sure ? Come, come ! There must be something wrong with you, some spiritual blight perhaps. . . .

Don't tell us that owing to a slight squint your eye invariably lights on the year's *second* whatever-it-is. This is no subject for jesting, and that was a Test Question we put to you. The point is—if you don't get shivers of delight up and down the spinal cord whenever you're gardening ; if you don't burn with gardenious affection, till your vest begins to smell scorched, at the mere thought of the year's first *Michausia Tchihatcheffi* ; in fact, if you're not plumpotty about the whole sobgoblinatious affair, what the Weevil do you mean by attempting to be a Gardener at all ?

Take it from us, it is utterly forbidden to be half-hearted about Gardening. *You have got to LOVE your garden, whether you like it or not.*

If you doubt this for a moment, how do you account
for the fact that all the Gardening Encyclopædias,
Diaries, Manuals, Articles, Magazines, and even (alas)
the Seedsmen's Catalogues are unanimously addressed
to GARDEN-LOVERS ?

There is simply no literature, no help, and evidently
no hope for people who merely *like* having a garden,
or don't mind if they do, or, fatalistically, just *have*
a garden.

To LOVE your garden is the one perennial Rule.
The *Golden Rule* Dean Nuisance calls it, though Capt.
Pontoon for some reason insists on referring to it as
the *Rule of Twee* and explains it (alas) as follows :
" Only by getting into a frenzy of horticultural smother-
love can a promoted window-box wallah *blind himself*
to the endless *anxieties, disappointments, lumbago* and
waste of valuable time involved in Gardening." " For
Love," adds that untrustworthy officer, " is always
blind ; like my old Scotch Gardener." [1]

*   *   *

In the following pages, therefore, we offer to every
demi-gardener an unparalleled opportunity of putting himself or herself quickly and decisively to the
Test.

For we propose (by kind permission of the Dean)
to take you right through all the essential parts
of gardening, sparing you nothing, not even the
Succulents.

And if at any point your Love falters ; if, for in-

[1] See *A Realist's Garden*, p. 74 *et seq.*, by Capt. W. D. Pontoon,
author of *Dirigible Quadrupeds, With Moss Bros. at Ascot*, and other
unsporting books.

stance, you fail to adore all Mr. Knatchbull Twee's lovely Thoughts (which we shall quote unsparingly) or start taking sides with Capt. Pontoon against Dean Nuisance, you will know (alas) that you are Unworthy of *The Garden Beautiful*, A Weed upon the fair face

of the Earth, a Human Plantain, and had better stay indoors and hide your head in a seedsman's catalogue for ever. . . .

On the other hand, if you come through the Test with a riot of flying colours, you will know that you are a certified sobgoblinatious gardener, in fact The Real Thing.

Think what that means ! It means that you have only to wear the right kind of silk jumper and practise

preening and pruning around in the right postures,
and some Press photographer may definitely mistake
you for Mr. Knatchbull Twee himself! It means that
you are well down the path to becoming as hardy and
perennial as Dean Nuisance himself, and may even
live to beat his world record of a Hundred and One
Blameless Books on Gardening, and Gardening, and
Gardening, and Gardening. . . .

Incidentally, you will be God's gift to a hundred
and two Tested Seedsmen (including the double-dutch
bulb-mongers) and to the cutthroat manufacturers
of a hundred and three species of Lovable Garden
Implements.

SPIT THE SECOND

PLANNING THE MODEST PLOT

*" Only at the behest of the provident will our Mother Earth yield
up her benison of bud and blossom."*
DEAN NUISANCE (The Garden Bountiful.).

" Your garden is your own funeral."
CAPT. PONTOON (Monday Morning in my Garden.).

IN order to make a clean start (you'll get dirty
enough before you're through) let us imagine that at
present your modest plot is not a garden at all, only
a flattish place of the usual oblong shape, on which
in theory it will be possible to grow things some
day——

What next? Well, all the best Garden Books and

even some real gardens begin with a *plan*. It is time you started planning the plot, or at least plotting the plan. So take a modest piece of foolscap (*Hieratica*

Basildonii) and plot out a modest list of all the things you will require in your garden.

THE MODEST PLAN

1. You will certainly require a herbaceous border, a lawn, a box-hedge, a rosery, a gravel path and a rockery.

2. It is usual nowadays to have a crazy pavement, a sundial, some terra-cotta dwarves and a flagstaff, or at least a pole for the wireless.

3. Your wife will demand a kitchen-garden, an orchard, a garden-seat, a sandpit for the children and a lovely goldfish pool (with water lilies).

4. You yourself would like a spot of topiary, a rain-gauge, a eucalyptus tree, a putting links, and a lovely pagoda—like the one at Kew only smaller, if necessary. (It was Mr. Knatchbull Twee's Idea, but you cribbed it, you wicked thing.)

5. Neighbours would be impressed if you had a tennis-court, a croquet-field, and, if they can recognize one, a Pleasaunce.

6. The bottom of the garden will inevitably become an *Unpleasaunce*, centring round a bonfire emplacement ; so, to make up for that, how about a gazebo, a haha, a rhododendron-drive, and a vinery—they give tone to a Place ?

7. Meanwhile, the children are clamouring for a see-saw, a goat, a hee-haw, a swing, a bathing-pool, a Zoo, and a monkey-puzzle.

8. Everyone, of course, has a shrubbery, and a summer-house, though (according to Capt. Pontoon) no one has the slightest idea what for.

9. A tool-shed is essential, and some deck-chairs (to put in the summer-house) and a ' rustic table ' (for wood-lice to get into the bark of).

10. You will never achieve a *blaze of colour* unless you have a *greenhouse*, some *green fingers* and of course a huge *orange-and-blue umbrella*.

11. Knatchbull (Mr. Twee) did just suggest a lotus-grove, and a fountain, and a statue of Priapus (or at least of Peter Pan).

12. And the Dean would be delighted to ' chance upon ' a Primrose Path—leading (of course) to the everlasting bonfire. . . .

You see, planning is not so easy after all ; one way and another there seem to be rather a lot of things to fit into your teeny-weeny acre ; one way and another (remember, you are *on trial*) there seem to be rather a lot of things to *Love*.

Are you quite sure, for instance, that you can love the sundial, the gazebo, the flagstaff, your wife and the monkey-puzzle, all at once, all the time, all with the same frenzied devotion ?

(Or would it be safer to chuck gardening and concentrate on your wife, the children, and the Chancellor of the Exchequer ?)

We are reminded (alas) of Gertrude Jekyll's tersely brilliant comment : " *In garden arrangement one has not only to acquire a knowledge of what to do, but to gain some wisdom in perceiving what it is well to let alone.*"

And of Angus MacFungus's verbose but even more inspired ejaculation " *Mony a mickle mucks a mackle* " (for ejaculating which once too often he was piped off the estate by the Earl of MacMuckle in 1883).

And even if you feel bung-full of love for Everything, hadn't you better just glance for a tiny second at your dwarf-income and your teeny-weeny Bank Balance ?

You agree ? Very well, then. Let us sharpen our pencil (as the Dean would say) and set about Thinning Out the Plan, Cutting back our Hopes, and Pruning Ambition, for as the dear Dean observes (" Life's Little Difficulties ", page 843) : " *If we cannot culti- vate Economy within our little plot we shall assuredly cultivate little else* ", and, as Angus MacFungus says, " *Wha canna thole wi' mickle maks unco' muckle dree.*" (A. MacFungus, Collected Meaningless Sayings of, un- published—touch wood.)

SPIT THE THIRD

PRUNING THE PLAN

SUBJECT to your approval we submit the following consolidation or concentration of the Plan, by means of which we hope you will be able to gratify most of your ambitions, and the good Dean, without having to purchase the whole County :

I. (*a*) Cancel goldfish pool (with lilies).
   (*b*) Concentrate goldfish (less lilies) in rain-gauge.
   (*c*) Put rain-gauge in fountain.
   (*d*) Now push fountain into summerhouse.

   Bravo !

II. (*a*) Plant monkey-puzzle in bathing-pool.
    (*b*) Place garden-seat under monkey-puzzle.
    (*c*) Consolidate bathing-pool in centre of croquet-pitch (new game—water-croquet).

    Well pruned !

III. (*a*) Store sundial in pagoda.
     N.B. Before doing this, tear off dial, cement on to own head, thus enabling self to bow to neighbour and ask for right time with some hope of getting right answer.
     (*b*) Think carefully about pagoda. Visualize pagoda. Gradually regret pagoda. For pagoda read *pergola*.

     Well read, Sir !

IV. Superimpose (*a*) Putting-links on croquet-lawn.
                     (*b*) Croquet-green on tennis-lawn.
                     (*c*) Tennis-lawn on lawn.

      Note.—If, later on, unsporting tennis players
           complain of catching their feet in the
           croquet-hoops and falling into the bath-
           ing-pool, or spraining their ankles in the
           golf-holes, point out firmly that *it isn't
           cricket.*

V. (*a*) Wring out eucalyptus tree on to lump of sugar.
   (*b*) Throw away husk.
   (*c*) Give sugar to snivelling children.

                                     Well thinned !

VI. Either (*a*) Store gazebo and haha in library
                  for use in cross-word puzzles.
    or (*b*) Wrap up haha, terra-cotta dwarves,
                  flag-staff, see-saw, rustic table and
                  all other nuisances (including Dean
                  Nuisance) in the gazebo and sacrifice
                  them to Priapus on the bonfire
                  emplacement.   Heil Hitler !

Ask for the right time.

SPIT THE FOURTH

WHAT'S LEFT IN THE PICTURE?

" Having laid out the Garden, the next thing is to lay out the gardener."
CAPT. PONTOON (*Pistils for Two*, p. 55).

HAVING thus eliminated some rather unlovable rubbish you are left, as a practical gardener, with a herbaceous border, a rockery, a rose-garden, a kitchen-garden, a greenhouse, a tool-shed, a cold-frame, a pergola, a box hedge, a primrose path, an Unpleasaunce (including bonfire emplacement) and a novelty Combination-lawn.

The swing, the orchard, the sandpit and the umbrella will, of course, have to be accommodated on the Combination-lawn somewhere near the bathing-pool, which, you will remember, now contains the monkey-puzzle and the garden seat.

Perhaps the best thing for you to do next would be to draw a picture of the result below and see how much you love it. Or alternatively see Fig. i overleaf and see how much you love that.

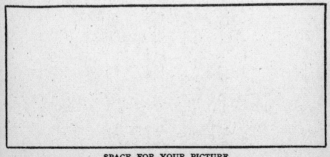

SPACE FOR YOUR PICTURE

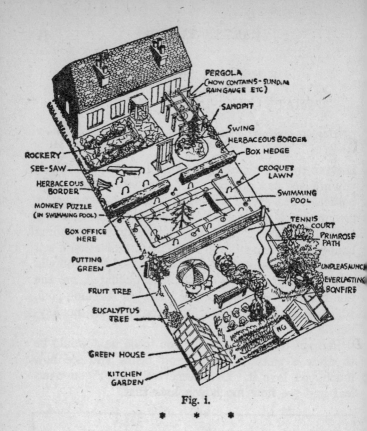

PERGOLA
(NOW CONTAINS - SUNDIAL
RAIN GAUGE ETC)

SANDPIT

SWING

HERBACEOUS BORDER

BOX HEDGE

CROQUET
LAWN

SWIMMING
POOL

TENNIS
COURT

PRIMROSE
PATH

UNPLEASAUNCE

EVERLASTING
BONFIRE

ROCKERY

SEE-SAW

HERBACEOUS
BORDER

MONKEY PUZZLE
(IN SWIMMING POOL)

BOX OFFICE
HERE

PUTTING
GREEN

FRUIT TREE

EUCALYPTUS
TREE

GREEN HOUSE

KITCHEN
GARDEN

Fig. i.

*   *   *

DIGRESSION

AH WILDERNESS !

SOME THOUGHTS AROUSED

BY

A DISTANT PROSPECT

OF

THE UNPLEASAUNCE

"WELL, that's all there is to see, we'll go back now. . . ."

Your hostess is lying to you. She knows perfectly well, and so do you, that there is just one more bit to see and that she doesn't want you to see it—that dreary devastated area, the skeleton in every gardenswanker's cupboard, the Glamis-monster of her domain ; in a word, *The Unpleasaunce*.

Every fair-sized garden has one (it is a Law of Nature) and one Unpleasaunce is much like another : they differ only in the number and variety of Depressing Things they harbour.

Similarly, every fair-sized garden-writer has a *Speciality*, and since all the other opportunities for displaying erudition (including Alpine Plants, Miletian Orchidaceæ, Never-flowering Shrubs, and Absolutely Poisonous Succulents) have been done to death by other writers, we shall treat you to a fair-sized treatise on the Speciality which we have been obliged to embrace, namely, *Things which Occur in the Unpleasaunce*.

You will be glad to know that our treatise, instead of being choked up with unpronounceable and wrongly derived Latin names, is all about things which, we hope, will be full of significance for the thousands of people who can hardly speak Latin at all but can recognize an Unpleasaunce all right when they see one.

Common or garden-writers' lack of modesty compels us to let you know that in the course of our Special Researches we have investigated hundreds of gardens, right to the bitter end. We are, quite frankly, the only world experts in Unpleasauntness.

THINGS WHICH OCCUR IN THE UNPLEASAUNCE
(*Our Speciality*)

(i) *Utilities.*

At its best (which it never is) the Unpleasaunce is full of things someone-forgot-he-had-plenty-and-ordered-more-of ; virgin pea-sticks, for instance, and barren seeding boxes, besides those little heaps of clinkers, slaked-lime, leaf-mould, pot-crocks, silver-sand, and soot—all the tedious cosmetics of The Garden Beautiful.

(ii) *Futilities.*

At its worst, the Unpleasaunce presents itself as the Mecca of the Unmentionables. In it will be found that small pit for throwing things into (caused by someone's desire to throw things into a small pit) which is always half-full of disembowelled fruit-tins, senile dish-clouts, condemned mouse-traps, bald scrubbing-brushes and stricken jampots, pickle-jars and stone-ginger bottles innumerable, all doubtless aspiring to eventual manure-dom and meanwhile giving rise to clouds of up-and-down midges at dusk, and places in the sun for squadrons of ink-striped blue-bottle flies and iridescent green-bottle flies.

There is usually a busted sieve somewhere in the Unpleasaunce and a devastated enamel kettle, and a rusted boot (keeping a tongueless vigil) with a docken growing out of it ; and, lying in the long grass, a heavy plank with plenty of woodlice underneath where the grass (like Mr. Knatchbull Twee's face) is all flattened out and anæmic, and half a symbolical ladder of success (with practically no rungs).

(iii) *Flora.*

Things grow in the Unpleasaunce of course : young grass out of an old doormat, voluntary vegetable marrows, parvenu pumpkins, and a riot of rogue rhubarb. And in every untrampled corner strong self-made borders of *Hurtica dioica*, the hardy perennial stinging-nettle.

(iv) *Fauna.*

No doubt there are rats, (but only at night when no one would have the nerve to investigate an Unpleasaunce); which probably accounts for the inevitable Abandoned Cat, which is always very pleased to see you—but not of course for the occasional Devastated Goat, which isn't.

There is often a wasps' nest in the Unpleasaunce. For offset, there is always a bonfire (which annoys the wasps) smouldering sourly alongside the heap of dejected grass-cuttings and adding vastly to the general Unpleasauntness.

(v) *Architecture.*

Here be also Erections. A rusty grindstone without a handle, and a scarred trestle for chopping and sawing things on, now almost hacked through, and a deserted

hutch for rabbits or possibly guinea-pigs, with a rent in the hexagonal wire-netting through which doubtless the beasts escaped—it is pleasing to know that they didn't starve to death.

But the architectural feature of all Unpleasaunces is the mysterious little *Shed*, grey outside and black inside, which no one has the courage to explore on account of the peculiar and distressing smell which seems to be its only inhabitant.

We can offer no explanation of this Shed or of the remarkable substance (apparently damp blotting-paper dipped in tar) with which it, and the rabbit-hutch too, is habitually cowled.

Among other possible erections are the *congé'd* cold frame, now framing nothing but a growth of giant artichoke, and the culverin-shaped Pump whose ankle wears a puttee made of bleached sacking tied with string and plugged with rotting straws. It is impossible to pump the pump because the handle has broken off and gone to join the other rusty things, the superannuated rakes and assorted prongs, the scarlet sawblade and the brown saw-like scythe-blade that lurk in the long grass in the hope of giving someone lock-jaw.

(vi) *Historical Exhibits.*

Here in the Unpleasaunces of England the backwash of recent history waits patiently for its absorption into the soil, and many are the period objects observed with astonishment by the authors on their tours of investigation.

Among those noted. Period wooden washstand (yellow period) partly devarnished, the plateau boldly pierced with bevelled holes for basin, carafe, toothmug and soapdish. Bottomless portmanteau (period 1860) neatly boxing-in a fine growth of flowering nettle and supporting on its inner sides serried wavelengths of horrible fungi. Skeleton of umbrella (period uncertain). Filthy old high-buttoning period waistcoat (1902). Ditto abdicated (crownless) straw-hat hastening to humify. Ostracized bead-curtain (recent).

Prize Discovery : oil-painting of genuine ancestor of last owner but three—this was found *in the Shed*.

(vii) *Mysteries*.

Some Extraordinary Objects which have been known to occur at the fag-ends of gardens. The back half of a dinghy :—? the result of a dissolved fishing partnership (Maida Vale '35). A rusticated bedstead with brass knobs and devastated mattress complete (Banstead '32). Whole kitchen-range (extinct). Full-sized unattached enamel bath with stuck taps and a little dark green slimy water at the bottom (Reigate and several other places). Stellenbosched sewing-machine (period ? 1908). Motor-car *upside-down* (near Wallingford)—Query : How it got there (no road in sight) and who was strong enough, gay enough or angry enough, to overthrow it ? Similarly, what of the enormous rusty cog-wheels so often encountered miles from the nearest factory, and the light railway tip-truck perched on a pile of rail-lengths, all obviously indestructible and now irremovable (Godalming district '34) ? And what,

yes *what* about the retired goldfish we found living
amid the dock-leaves near Wantage, in a porcelain
enamel lavatory cistern and groundless terror of the
plug being pulled any minute.

(viii) *Fear and Hatred of the Unpleasaunce.*

Melancholy from any point of view, the Unpleasaunce
is capable of arousing emotions of Fear and Hatred.
Hatred of the Unpleasaunce is stronger among towns-
folk, who think it is just a piece of slovenliness on the
gardener's part (like a housemaid who brushes all the
' flue ' under the sofa) than among gardeners, who
know that it is a partly justifiable phenomenon and
in any case an absolutely inevitable one.

Countrymen fear the Unpleasaunce. They know
that if it is not ruthlessly kept down and cut back it
will *encroach* : pushing out tentacles like an Octopus—
a rusty hoe here, a sub-bonfire there, an advance-guard
of nettles, an outpost of rhubarb—it will begin to
infiltrate, to creep along the hedges towards the house
in an attempt to oversmother the whole estate.

Many a garden-lover has woken up shuddering in
the still hours and rushed to the window to make sure
that his Unpleasaunce-Nightmare (well known to all
psychoanalysts) was only a dream. That the garden is
still there. That the Unpleasaunce—which he had
dreamt was surging ungovernably across the lawn,
grubbing its way up the steps of the loggia, fumbling
at the French windows and even starting to climb up
on the shoulders of the Virginia Creeper in order to
join forces with the box-room, the nursery, the housemaid's cupboard and other internal unpleasaunces, for
a final assault and conquest of the whole house—that

the Unpleasaunce is still in its proper place at the far
end of the kitchen-garden ; as beastly as ever, doubtless, but still, thank heavens, held at bay. . . .

*It is a terrible thought, that if ever the gardening-
classes lose courage and give up their gallant and perennial
struggle with these monsters, within a year the whole of
England will be one vast and permanent Unpleasaunce.*

SPIT THE FIFTH

EARTH CONTROL

" There are more things in Heaven and Earth . . ."
HAMLET.

" I want to be a loam ! "
GRETA GARBO.

AND now to return to The Plan.   It is well worth looking at, on paper.   Like all Garden Plans (there are
thousands being plotted all over England at this
moment) it is really quite Lovable—on paper !

It almost seems a pity not to leave it like that : it
is so much cleaner and neater and less infested with
pests than it will ever be again.

But that would not be considered Good Gardening
and the Love wouldn't count.   Sooner or later if you
take gardening seriously, unlike the people who merely
dibble in it, you must start *making* your garden.

Your impulse will probably be to start by putting
one of the *deck-chairs* under the *orange umbrella* and
sitting in it—just to see if it is in good working order.
But that would be a false start.   The thing you have
got to do first, is *to find out what sort of soil you are on.*

There are hypothetically five different kinds of soil:

(1) *Clay.* Strong, tenacious stuff; excellent for cultivating roses; clings magnificently to boots, spades, socks, etc., so that garden is gradually transferred to tool-shed, boot-scraper or own bedroom, or sent in weekly instalments to the laundry. In hot weather clay becomes bricks; in cold weather, ice-cream bricks.

(2) *Sand.* Delightful for digging in, especially at the seaside in August; but *too porous to retain moisture*. Reinforce with old cabbage-stalks, caramels, chewing-gum, etc., or insert suet-dumplings and old sponges at intervals of 6 inches. Or spread huge mackintosh carpet underneath whole garden.

(3) *Chalk.* Dairy farmers may appreciate it as useful foil to cheese; but on a pure chalk soil nothing will grow. Two possible remedies: (i) grow nothing; (ii) filch someone else's garden and mulch it down on top of your own (see p. 44, Transmigration of Soils).

(4) *Flint.* The chief objections to a flinty soil are the flints. Collect these and throw them over the wall into neighbour's garden. But the more you throw away the more will appear. Two explanations of this: (i) The flints *breed underground* (all peasants believe this).

(ii) Your neighbour is unsporting and
throws them back again every night.
(Probably a Dirty Foreigner/Jew/Fas-
cist / Bolshevik / Pedestrian / Nudist /
Buchmanite/Troglodyte.) [1]

(5) *Loam.*   *The ideal soil is a " rich unctuous loam ".*
This however is *never found* (except in
the gardens of rich unctuous people, or
possibly in the garden of those frightful
people next-door).

What's Yours ?

Even so, these are all theoretical soils, that is to say
somebody has got some soil like that somewhere, *but
not you.*

We will now have to investigate the composition of
some real, inevitable, absolutely pathetical suburban
soil like yours.

We find that an acre of average real practical soil
actually contains :

Coke	8%
Centipedes	100%
Oxidized Metal (sardine-metal, cisterns, bottle-openers, buttons, etc.)	10%
Moist Impenetrable Sacking	5%
Other fibrous matter (braces, corsets, decayed hosiery, etc.)	19%
American Oilcloth	2%
Hidden Treasure (Diamonds, Doubloons, Roman Coins, Cheques to Bearer).	*None*
Stones (including Limestones, Grimestones, Tombstones, Plumstones, Old Red Sandstones, and ordinary Giant Landstones)	20%

[1] Cross out all except the one you happen to Hate.

Fossilized Bowler Hats	.	.	.	.	7%
Bicycle tyres, corks, cinders and sundries				.	17%
Etruscan Ceramics, drain-pipes, false teeth and other crockery		.	.	.	. 8%
Historic footwear	.	.	.	.	. 25%

? 343%

Seen through a microscope it appears thus:

1 Acre of average soil seen under powerful microscope.

Very well. Somehow or other you have simply got to acquire some of that *rich unctuous loam*.

There are only three methods. One is to curry favour with a rich unctuous uncle, dig yourself well into his confidence and secure a rich unctuous loan of £500.

Alternatively, since everything (even old bowlers, braces, and razor-blades) can ultimately be transformed into valuable soil *by worms*, you can lay down and squelch-in a huge quantity of worms (say 5,000,000) and leave them to do their stuff, or as Dean Nuisance would say " to fulfil their function as the agents of Nature's beneficent handiwork ". The process, however, is slow. Darwin states that it takes 7,000,000 worms 14 years to chew over one acre of period grey bowlers (any period) and another 7 years to turn the fibrous residuum into an undeniable unctuum.

Obviously, something must be done quickly! So perhaps you had better fall back on Prof. Heath

The Transmigration of Soils.

Robinson's method of *Transference by Suction.* For this all that is required is a hole in the garden wall, a vacuum-cleaner, a conviction that the end justifies the means and a dark and stormy night. The object

of the latter being, of course, to drown the drooling
of the vacuum-cleaner in the droning of the wind.

SPIT THE SIXTH

MANURIAL RITES

I. HUMUS

" All really grim gardeners possess a keen sense of Humus."
CAPT. PONTOON.

Do not imagine, however, that having secured the
unctuous loam and having spread it evenly over the
garden, you have merely to sit down and watch
the onions and moon-daisies pooping up out of it in
unctuous bloom. Your soil, remember, like other
objects of unearned affection (such as roses, husbands,
children, and Old Scotch Gardeners) is a *gross feeder*.
Soil in fact must be *lovingly and continually nourished*,
and the thing you feed it on, chiefly, is called HUMUS.

On the other hand, all garden-lovers are used to
having difficult English names explained to them by
simple Latin sentences, e.g. Forget-me-not (*myosotis
boraginaceæ*) and are consequently aware that the
word *Humus*, found in all Latin dictionaries, means
simply, SOIL.

This is of course a typical snobgoblinatious garden
mystery; but it does help to explain the warning,
found in all Garden books, that " *Soil* which is totally
lacking in *Humus* is TOO THIN, and of absolutely no
practical value. . . ."

II. DING

" Nature is divinely ordained and in her service the lowliest things are high."

DEAN NUISANCE (*Trowels and Tribulations*).

However, the books go on to say that the way to provide the garden with Humus is to lay in a huge

Ding Heil !

supply of richly decayed farmyard manure—or " Ding," as Angus MacFungus so obstinately calls it (Mr. Knatchbull Twee infinitely prefers the term " Dressing ").

There is nothing in the whole realm of gardening

which arouses so much pride and adoration or, if it
belongs to your neighbour, so much envy and all
uncharitableness, as a really vast stack of crusty, well-
matured, asphyxiating, Vintage *Ding*. And it is only
natural that an object of so much horticultural devotion
should, like Humus, be surrounded with (as it were)

an aura, or (as it actually is) an aroma, of considerable
mystery.

For it is one of the oldest and quite the most baffling
of the Manurial Laws that *the longer you keep manure
the shorter it becomes!*

This is not because covetous people keep penetrating
into your Unpleasaunce (where the Ding is stacked)
and stealing the top layer; it is just another of the
technical mysteries deliberately introduced into Garden-

ing (by Reginald Farrer or someone) to make it more
difficult ; and the long and the short of it is that manure
which has *been kept a short time* is mysteriously called
" *long manure* " and *vice versa !*

Nauseating, of course, but manure is like that—the
higher the shorter, the longer the cheaper ; and yet,
as Mr. Twee apologetically protests, " always definitely
bloom-making ".

You will therefore, however much you hate other
people's manure, find no difficulty in worshipping your
own *Ding.*

III. SUBSIDIARY DRESSINGS

" Comparisons are odorous."
                                        SHAKESPEARE.

Most people know that any manure is revolting but
don't realize that practically anything revolting is
manure. For instance, practically anything from a
Tannery might be taken and mulched into the earth
to the general profit of the land, including probably
the beastly old Board of Directors.

It is therefore quite in order to mention one or two
of the more adorable Subsidiary Dressings. But since
in a field fraught with so much emotion comparisons
(as Shakespeare knew) are odorous, we shall do no
more than enumerate a few minor Manurial Rites
which you may have to perform, leaving all fine
distinctions to those who possess a real *flair* for the
thing.

(i)   Collect *oak leaves* and bury them in a hole in the

ground. Try to find hole again after six months or the Rite becomes a mere formality.

(ii) Plug cucumber beds with *guano*. *N.B.* Guano is a rather dressy little manure made from the cast-off dinner-jacket (or tuxedo) of the Peruvian Penguin or other peculiar South American Dickey-bird.

(iii) When you go to the seaside don't collect shells or peculiar postcards but large bunches of *seaweed*, and hang it up in the spare-room when you get home, till it is naught but fragrancy. If your guests object, remind them that *dried blood* is excellent for giving colour and texture to the soil—though between ourselves you are no longer allowed to kill people in order to get it.

(iv) *Pond Mud* should be collected in pockets of old gardening coat or subsidiary dressing-gown and slung at the garden in handfuls. Give due warning ("Ach-dung!" "Dung-ho!" etc.).

(v) On the other hand it is possible to *overdress* the soil, and the remedy is *Lime*. Only, the books usually advise the gardener to use Lime and Dressing *alternate years*, and, on the next page, always *to look a year ahead*—which confuses the mind and causes Ding-frustration, or, in alternate years, Lime-frustration. Other correctives are *bicarbonate of soda* (for acid soils), *potash* (obtained by burning wood, not by setting light to flower-pots), *basic slag* (you get this out of a volcano), *bonfire-refuse* and *soot*. So from every point of view it might be a good plan to set light to the garden alternate years and burn it to the ground.

(vi) There is a mysterious substance, found only in

a certain part of Germany, and called *Kainit*. But we cannot remember what you do with it, *Kursit*.

(vii) *Warning.* Anything which remains long enough in the Unpleasaunce will eventually become manure. So beware! *Don't stay too long in the Unpleasaunce yourself!*

SPIT THE SEVENTH

SOME FAVOURITE PESTS

> "*There be a mort o' voles hereabound.*"
> MARY WEBB.

"*AND now 'tis May-time, and the marauding grub . . .*" as Dean Nuisance remarks sooner or later in practically all his books; neglecting (alas) to reveal in any of them which exactly *is* the marauding grub.

Not that a small point like this matters when the subject is so multifarious. For, ever since horticulture became a science, scientists have been joyously discovering so many varieties of pests and breeding so many species of counter-pests that there are now probably more pests than scientists—or so it is estimated by statisticians and others who (like the pests) have the gift of multiplying rapidly.

And of course by taking a broad view and adding the scientists to the pests, and throwing in most of the writers of Garden Books, one could arrive at an absolutely astronomical total of horticultural handicaps.

Passionate pest-lovers will therefore forgive us, please, for mentioning only a few favourite garden pests—in the order we should like them exterminated, please—including possibly Mr. Knatchbull Twee and, alas, Dean Nuisance.

THEIR NATURE AND TREATMENT

To tell you the truth we are not sure whether it is your duty to love these bugs, beetles and other burrowing brutes or not. The Scriptures admonish us to love our enemies ; on the other hand Garden Literature is full of exhortations to " keep watch and ward ", etc., against all " garden foes " including the Marauding Grub (will no one tell us which grub that is ?) and are full of hints on how to destroy an ant, annoy a hornet, terrify a caterpillar, unhinge a snail, reduce a woodlouse to hysteria and make life tedious for mice ; in fact, how to quell anything except a riot of colour.

So perhaps your best compromise would be to try to *love the labour of doing-in the pests*, particularly the labour so daintily referred to as ' finger-and-thumb work '—in plain English, squashing the pulpy ones to death with your dainty hands. . . .

Finger-and-thumb work.

i. *Onion-fly.* A species of Fly which, being devoid of original ideas, attacks Onions. Withhold the Onion and the Fly dies. No need to be cruel : don't keep letting the fly see the onion. Take it right away and hide it.

ii. *The Woolly Aphis.* Send it to the Laundry. When it comes back send it to the wash again. After two or three goes it will shrink so tight on to itself that it will suffocate.

iii. *Wire-worm.* Easily distinguishable (like Mr. Knatchbull Twee) by its long slender yellowish body. Easily caught by burying slices of turnip (ground-bait) secured on a skewer. (But you can't catch Mr. Twee that way.)

iv. *Weevils.* Ignore them—remember the old warning " Hear no weevil, see no weevil, speak no weevil " and cut them dead.

v. *Cockchafer Grub.* Of a pasty white appearance (like Dean Nuisance) but (unlike the Dean) has a *bluish tail.* Paint the other end blue. Checkmate !

vi. *Potato-fly.* Even more dangerous to encounter

at dusk than a bull cockchafer practising for the Schneider Cup. Treat as you would treat a potato if it pestered you beyond endurance, i.e. choice of boiled, mashed, fried, or Buzz Off !

Potato fly.

vii. *Leather-jacket Grub.* Attacks roots of grass. Employ treachery, thus : Erect miniature cloak-room with minute pegs on edge of lawn. Before getting down to work, grubs will, naturally, hang up jackets. Now is your chance—confiscate all jackets—pneumonia —finish !

viii. *Cuckoo-spit.* The usual notices (40/-, £5, etc.) should be put up in the places the cuckoos spit from (usually near the rose-garden). *Note : Birds* are very destructive, especially in orchards and places where they sing, and *cannot be stamped out* (they move too quickly).

ix. *Greenfly.* Likes Roses. A splendid subject for snappy thumb-and-finger work, enabling you to acquire *green-fingers* in a few seconds without all the bother of having to inherit them.

x. *Blackcurrant Mite.* Risk it—it miten't.

xi. *Basic Slug.* Innumerable weighty pamphlets on slug-control are obtainable. Obtain a 10-lb. one. Read it out to slug. If slug doesn't play the game, slug it with the pamphlet.

xii. *Mildew.* Appearance—see Dean Nuisance's Umbrella. Treatment—watch and spray (preferably with a solution of quassia-may-call'ems and thin-gummy-chips).

xiii. *Mr. Knatchbull Twee.* In the words of that awful song, says Capt. Pontoon, only God can make a Twee ; and the Dean says it's fruitless to question the ways of Providence—so there we are. . . .

xiv. *Dean Nuisance.* At times we are tempted to look forward to the day when Death comes to Dean Nuisance. Meanwhile perhaps the next pest thing would be to look forward to p. 54, on which our subconscious artist has drawn an epic wish-fulfilment picture of this desirable occurrence.

Death comes to Dean Nuisance.

SPIT THE EIGHTH

WHAT'S THE IDEA?

" O to be in England now that Dean Nuisance is on a Hellenic Cruise."
CAPT. PONTOON.

THE question which now shoots up is, *why* exactly are you doing all this? Because Purposeless Gardening will get you nowhere (except into a state of all-over Unpleasaunce), and every true tenacious Garden Lover is expected to strive after one of the Recognized Ideals such as ' The Garden Beautiful ' or ' The Greenhouse Gay ' or the Sweet Pea *rather* Sweet (don't you think?) or perhaps nothing more ambitious than The Cold Frame Partially Intact or The Old Gardener Occasionally Sober (don't you believe it).

Though between you and us and the compost the activities of Garden Lovers can (alas) be far more objectively divided into four Recognizable Frenzies— the common object of which is clearly to weed out one's own inferiority complex and make the neighbours feel like worms—namely :

I. ROCK GARDENING

On the face of it, a rockery appears to be an attempt to pile up rocks and then hide them with invisible plants or to pile up invisible plants and then hide them with rocks.

The true purpose of rock-gardening, however, is to triumph over Nature as well as the neighbours by first making gardening as difficult as possible and then succeeding in growing minute flowers—tiny saxifrages, teeny febrifuges and weeny-weeny sweet-sarcophaguses —in the face of all the difficulties or even on the faces of all the rocks.

"Thus the main idea of the rock gardener is to produce a wonderful show of high-Alpine plants in a sunken garden, preferably at sea-level. Or perhaps by contemplating these outcrops of *freesia pontresina*, *phlox phunicula*, *tobogany* and the like, to delude himself into thinking that he is in Switzerland ; in which case provided he never goes to Switzerland he will be able to keep up the illusion."   (Capt. Pontoon.)

A wonderful show of Alpine plants.

Rock Gardening is in any case compulsory, because if you don't have a rockery you will be pestered all day by neighbourly *jungfraus* barging in on you with good advice, edelweiss, boasts, boulders and bunches of *Sweet Fanny Adams* from their own miniature Matterhorns.

But don't get carried away : don't order a whole mountain over from the Engadine complete with chamois, avalanches, glaciers and pine-forests careering up and down it.

Even the text-books say " be economical at first in the use of stone ". We agree: no use overdoing even that (see Fig. ii).

Fig. ii.

At the same time it's no good being cowardly: one stone with a single sprig of *Halitosis Carter Paterson* on the top and some moss round the base will only resemble a petrified Christmas pudding (see Fig. iii).

Another point: if you get *the stones too small* people will mistake your rockery for a pile of road-mending material and tramps will come and sit on it and eat things out of paper bags, and no one will get the Idea of being in Switzerland. While if you get *the stones too big* you will never be able to

Fig. iii.

move them from wherever the contractor first dumped them and your rock-garden will be permanently in the wrong place (see Fig. iv).

We could give you lots more good adweiss, such as 'start at the bottom' and 'insert a little earth before it's too late' and so on, but the really important things

Fig. iv.

to remember are (1) that a rockery *must* be designed to *represent something, in miniature*—say, the devastated area in Flanders 1918, or an Island in the Hebrides, e.g. Rum, or Eigg, or simplest of all, Muck ; and (2) that the most frenzied form of screemasonry is *Moraine Gardening* (briefly, imitating the devastated area left after a glacier has rushed by) which according to the experts is " best done at the foot of a steep cliff " (you may have to move your house for this) ; and (3) that the flowers will be *so small you can hardly see them*.

Indeed our ingenious friend Capt. Pontoon has thoughtfully installed a large magnifying glass tethered

by a chain to a post in his Alpine garden " to enable
my guests " as he puts it " to see the point."

II. POOPING THE COLOURS

*" . . . and largest of all Viscountess Gladsome, delicate mauve-pink,
flushed scarlet."*

GARDEN MANUAL.

A. *Parade Gardening*. Not to be confused with
Marine Parade Gardening, the all-embracing object of
which is to provide flirting-embrasures for the Visitors,
the Idea of Parade Gardening is to stage a sort of
horticultural tattoo with " scarlet tulips marching and
countermarching 'twixt the serried ranks of wall-
flower " or peradventure " frail cosmetick columbines
like slender mannequins asway . . ." (see your favourite
garden magazine).

The Idea, as is only too well known, lends itself to
original colour-screams such as ' a plethora of blood-
red geraniums interveined with sanguinary blue

lobelia '; and the only snag is that the parade is apt
to get out of control—resulting in what is (alas) only

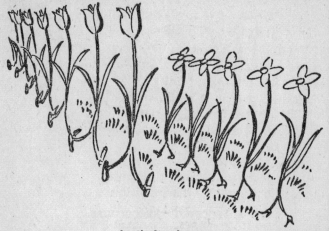

. . . horticultural tattoo . . .

too well known as 'a riot of colour' (? Anarchist
Gardening).

B. *Torch Gardening.* One of the Recognized Ideals
for Garden Lovers is 'The Herbaceous Border Ablaze
from June to October' (what a hope!), and the
Recognized Snag is that the 'herbs' *will not* come up
punctually and that the border is always asnag with
vexaceous gaps. . . .

"The remedy," says Captain Pontoon, "is to plug
the gaps by planting high-voltage Gladiolus bulbs;
and if the result is a complete black-out due to your
having accidentally plugged-in an onion, thus fusing
the whole garden, I can only suggest that you stare
fixedly at the blinding show of *Sweet William, Old
Harry* and *Eschscholtzia Hore-Belitzia* on page 10 of

your seedsman's catalogue and then suddenly transfer
the gaze to the nearest expanse of vacant soil.   As a
last resort you might try taking part of the garden and
looking at it through my special rose-tinted spectacles."
(See Fig. v.)

Fig. v.

But your desire to triumph over all other garden-
lovers is, we hope, so sincere that rather than descend
to such subterfuges, you would cheerfully abandon
the whole flaming thing and try some other Idea such
as—

III. GREENSWARDSMANSHIP

" I want to be a lawn."

GRETA GARBO.

" Too often, alas," writes the Good Dean, " a poor
and scraggy lawn serves but as a sorry adjunct to our

trim beds and well-stocked borders. Not thus shall we attain the Garden Beautiful."

Certainly notthus! Because the object of Green-swardsmanship is to acquire a Lawn (sorry! adjunct) so verdant that everyone goes green with envy at the sight of it. Consequently, even if you feel rather poor and scraggy yourself, you had better consider the few legitimate and legal methods of acquiring a genuine Greensward : namely, By Mort d'Ancestor, By Deed Turbary, By Phrenzy of Plantisede, or By Laches Plantigrade, all of which we will now explain (don't mention it).

(i) *Mort d'Ancestor.* The noblest way of acquiring a rich velvety greensward is to inherit one from a rich velvety ancestor. So if you think by any chance that you have been excluded by some legal trickery from the true ownership of, say, St. John's College, Oxford, or Hampton Court Palace, or all the best parts of the Wiltshire Downs, pop round and see your solicitors about it, remembering to bring some documents proving your legitimate descent from Cardinal Wolsey, The Abbot of Salisbury Plain, or, better still, the original Lord Ancestor.

(ii) *Deed Turbary.* " Only if he is possessed of a long purse," estimates the Dean, " can the gardener afford the luxury of laying down Turves," and it is possible that Captain Pontoon has the same idea in mind when he declares that " the starting-gate of all really expen-sive educations is the Turf ". So the first thing to do, if you decide to turf, is to get a tape-measure and work out the length of your purse against the square footage of the proposed Lawn. If, after all, you are left with a lawn which looks like this,

you will conclude that you have done the sum quite wrong, or that the children were unable to resist the appetizing appearance of the little chocolate Swiss rolls of turf delivered by the seedsman and have eaten quite a lot of them.

In either case your neighbours will be unable to resist the pleasure of pointing at the sorry adjunct and asking " What's that—Alopecia ? " and you will be obliged to buy a longer purse and start again, or dig the whole place over topsy-turvy-wise and then try method (iii).

(iii) *Phrenzy of Plantisede.* Sowing grass-seeds is cheaper and the children won't eat them (if they do, wait ten days, turn the little tiresomes inside out and turf them out on the lawn). But grass-sowing is so laborious that you have to be in a state of positively lovelawn frenzy before you can do it—as follows :

Dig up ground to a depth of at least 10 spits and pick out all thin sand, clay, boulders, fossilized bowler hats, etc. ; in fact remove whole front garden and throw it away, or give it to a hospital or something. Now plant drain-pipes 3 inches apart : this will serve as a solid foundation (or don't you think so ?). Fork in liberally peat-moss, pond-mud, and short stable-manure : rake over tyrannically with rough rake and roll flat (being careful not to trip over roller and fall flat on to rough rake). Now rake absolutely flat-out with fine rake and roll flatter (say, with flat roller). Stretch strands of black cotton cats-cradically to snare sparrows, self, etc. Set slug-traps, mouse-traps, man-traps, tank-traps, and (if you are a hopeless pessimist) dig deep holes for wild elephants to fall into.

Finally, if there is still time, *remember to sow some grass-seed*. But examine it first : if it proves to have been rhododendron seed, the results will be so different —so much bigger, for instance, and so much more difficult to roll. . . .

(iv) *Laches Plantigrade.* " No success attends the man who allows the grass to grow under his feet," says Dean Nuisance. Frankly, we think the Dean has gone too far : he has over-preached himself this time. What he says, although true of the herbaceous border, is entirely untrue of the lawn. Method (iv)—the static, pedological or plantigrade method—is really by far the simplest,

Fig. vi. Allowing grass to grow under your feet.

because all you have to do is to *stand perfectly still for a very long time, thus allowing the grass to grow under your feet.*

How quickly you get the lawn finished depends obviously on the size of your feet (see Fig. vi).

IV. CRAZY GARDENING

The purpose of Crazy Gardening (ord: *idiotici:* numerous species cultivated) is to triumph over such irritating things as Common Sense, Common Decency and those Common People next door. . . .

For instance everyone knows the standard form of Crazy gardening which consists in filling up half the garden with yards of crazy pavement and then, apparently, introducing a Gorgon's Head thus filling the rest of the garden with *fossilized gnomes, terra cotta dwarves, concrete rabbits, leaden birds, porcelain toadstools* and *cast-iron perpetual dogs* (*any breed, coloured to taste or spotted, per each* 7/6).

Scarcely less crazy is the mental blight known as *Pergalomania*, which consists in *total inability to stop making pergolas* (see pergolatrous garden on extreme left in picture on p. 26).

Little need be said—too much, alas, is known—about those crazy gardeners who show their doting affection for the garden by *taking it indoors* (not accidentally on their boots, but deliberately in pots) filling with bowls full of rich wet composts every cupboard, drawer and wardrobe in the spare bedroom (" you won't be unpacking much, will you ? "), damping off their rare brackens and other herbal parafernalia in all the washbasins, and even attempting to grow mushrooms under the bath.

Worse still are Whimsical Gardeners who go in for " Pinch Gardens ", i.e. gardens stocked exclusively with seedlings they have pinched, and label each specimen accordingly, e.g. *Primula Mr. & Mrs. Smith*, 109 *Acacia Road : Royal Anemone Chelsea Show* 1935 ; *Banana, Kew* 1936 : *Orchid Messrs. Floradora Ltd.*, 198, *Piccadilly : Pink Geranium Clodsham Station*, 9.54 *Sundays only, Paddington first stop*. (List kindly supplied by Lady Cheter Whimsey.)

Other well-known follies are Matrimonial Gardening, meaning the arrangement of whimsical marriage-beds, such as *Hibiscus Count Zeppelin* with (alas) *Calceolaria Charlotte Brontë*, or a tasteful bed of *Celibacy Cardinal Manning* relieved by splashes of *Auricula Purple Bedder* (the old maudlin Oxford variety)—and Alphabetical Gardening, or growing flowers in the form of letters, e.g. abbreviations of institutions you admire, like T.U.C., C.I.D., or initials of former sweethearts and favourite creditors—the only justifiable form being Rly. Stn. Gardening, which tells you so pleasantly (' Say it with flowers ') the full name of the station you ought to have got out at.

Finally we note the Collecting Mania which compels quixotic evergreen-snobs to accumulate exotic nevergreen-shrubs (however melancholy), or to cultivate the strangest possible flowers in the wrongest possible places

—Thibetan poppies in Thames Ditton and Borneo orchids at Bournemouth.

But of all these eccentrics surely the most bewitched are those who go in for *cactus*-growing, or, as the philo-succulents themselves say, " embrace the Cactus."

Their excuse, no doubt, is that it is the most searing test of one's capacity to love any Green Thing however hideous, tedious, or dangerous, because (i) though not all prickly plants are cactuses (old proverb ' all that prictus is not cactus ') most succulent plants defend themselves by either pricking you (see Fig. vii) or

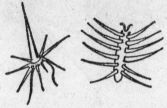

Fig. vii. Some things you may come up against. . . .

poisoning you, or both, (ii) they are all designed to grow in the endless sunshine of the Arizona Deserts and *not* in the dampish twilight of a Dulwich Conservatory, (iii) " there are 124 genera and 2000 species " (Britton & Rose) and " there is nothing so depressing as a lot of sick cacti " (Vera Higgins) and " she's telling us " (Capt. Pontoon), (iv) they take six years to grow six inches, and ' flower ' for one night only, usually as a sign of impending calamity, with the exception of the Mexican Cereus which grows sixty feet in six weeks and poisons you whenever you look at it (or even think of it), (v) they are practically all designed to dishearten their Lovers by a close resemblance to something utterly frightful—a German saw bayonet, the Brobdingnagian wax models of lice found in Natural History Museums, green lobsters, Mills bombs, barbed wire, long-haired bogeys, spiked clubs for trench-raiders, surrealist sweetmeats, a cross between a hedgehog and a fircone, or The Undying Worm. . . .

Worse still in the course of sixty years or so your Cactus-lover tends to get more and more like the

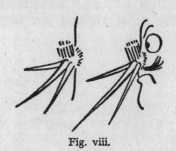

Fig. viii.

objects of his devotion (see Fig. viii). So if you decide to become a Phyllo-succulent you must be prepared to

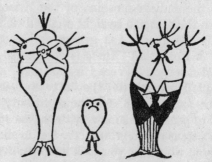

Mr. & Mrs. P Succulent and Child.

live in terror of growing sixty feet in a night and gradually becoming so hideous, tedious, poisonous, etc., that everyone will recognize you as a portent of personal or even of international calamity. . . .

SPIT THE NINTH

MANUAL LABOURS

" No idle man ever became a real gardener."
DEAN NUISANCE.

" Or a real nuisance."
CAPTAIN PONTOON.

WHATEVER form of gardening you go out for, you will inevitably be let in for nearly all of the nine Perpetual Labours which we have specially selected from nine hundred Hardy Manuals of Popular Gardening and pricked out for you on the next few pages.

DIGGING AND TRENCHING

" O pardon me, thou bleeding piece of earth."
SHAKESPEARE.

Many gardeners spend day after day, just digging— apparently in search of soil, though if they kept their eyes open they would in our opinion find any amount of soil, right on the surface.

Trenching (intensive or demoniac soil-hunting) consists of digging up the garden, spitting three feet deep, and putting it back again upside-down, thus—begin by digging out the whole of the earth out of a hole (in the earth) ; then dig out another hole and put the whole of it into the first hole. Go on like this, if you like, till you have dug up the whole of The Earth . . . but *when you get to the end* you will always find *you're in a hole* ; and the way to get out of it is to put it in a barrow and take it to *the other end* and fit it carefully under The Earth . . . (*N.B.*—Avoid treading on the diggings or you will have to do the hole doings all over again.)

Whole-trenching is a very ancient rite, so consider yourself lucky to have an up-to-date spade to do it with, and not a mediæval delving-iron (see Fig. ix.)

Fig. ix.

Half-trenching or " *bastard-trenching* " (as it is, alas, sometimes called) is exactly half as beastly, or according to Mr. Knatchbull Twee, " not *quite* so *nice* ". We therefore attach about half a beastly diagram (see Fig. x) revealing the primary stage in half-trenching :

Fig. x.

Soil (at A) 10 inches deep and one yard wide must be dug out and removed to far end of trench. Subsoil (at B) is likewise dug out and turned over, lovingly, with trench-tools. Enemy (at Bay) are in dug-out 10 yards East of Parapet (P). Zero hour 5.30 ack emma . . . and hoping this finds you pink in the face as it leaves us at present. . . .

SOWING

A. *In Open Beds and Borders.*

The boring bit in Sowing is, undoubtedly, the Drill. Get this right, as follows :

1. Buy threepenny packet of, say, Iceland Poppy seed. Rattle packet childishly and croon over colour-

ful exterior depicting Iceland Poppy in full bloom
(probably in Iceland).   Note also leaking corner-joints
of packet through which seed pours out into cupboard,
coat-pocket, etc

2. Prepare soft, well-decayed, old-loamy bed (for
seed, not self).   Put on well-decayed old loamy
trousers.   Get down to it and sow seed.

(*Note.*—Prospectus on packet says, " Sow in the open
from March to May ", but it is not really necessary to
go on as long as that.)

3. Rise to surface when blood runs to head and
survey handiwork, knee-cap craters, etc. (see Fig. xi).

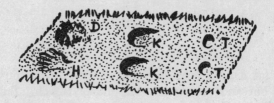

Fig. xi.

H=handiwork, performed by left hand.
K=knee-cap craters.
T=toe-cap craters.
D=boring attempted by dog to improve soil by
    addition of bone-meal.

4. Try again, adopting Colossus of Rhodes attitude
over seed-bed, until head runs to seed (see Fig. xii).

5. Ensure immediate blaze of colour by tying colour-
ful packet to stake, and protect seed-rows with knitted-
wire tunnels.   After a week, tiny green shoots will
appear : these are (alas) Iceland chickweed : destroy.

Later, if sinister little white snakes rear their heads,
spare them : because (i) they are not wire-worms

Fig. xii.

coming up to devour the tuppeny bars of wirework but *the seedlings,* (ii) it will be an absolute miracle—what the Dean so rightly calls *the miracle of growth from seed.*

B. *Sowing under Glass.*

Place in a well-washed seed-box one layer well-washed old crocks, one layer rough stuff, one layer well-squashed compost of sifted loam.

(*N.B.*—Bottom of seed-box must be carefully ventilated with holes made by v. skilful method (alas, not yet invented) so that air can get in but soil can't get out.)

Resist temptation to pause and gaze prophetically into the fuchsia, and note that so far you have omitted to put any seeds in.

If by some miracle (or mango-trick) seedlings (or mangoes) eventually appear, prepare fresh old crocks and new rich composts, shuffle seedlings frenziedly from one receptacle to another and harden them gradually by pricking-out, damping-off, hitting-back, potting the red, etc. After a few months of this mucking-about it will be a miracle if you're not an old crock yourself and definitely *non compost mentis*.

SPECIAL NOTE.   FLOWER-POT PSYCHOLOGY

Old crocks are made by bashing flower-pots joyfully

against the garden wall. Our researches reveal (1) criminal tendency to make far more old crocks than are required ; (2) widespread ignorance among green-hussifs as to what hole in floor of flower-pot is for ; (3) widespread waste of time on futile experiments such as seeing which finger fits best into hole in floor of flower-pot ; (4) that all flower-pots of a certain age and standing contain one cobweb and at least one dried scratchy leaf, and (5) that next to smashing flower-pots, the most popular vice is *risking it* by performing well-known Covent Garden *tour de force* or Pagoda trick (see Fig. xiii).

Fig. xiii.

PLANTING, ETCETERA

Of all the numberless named varieties of Dishonesty that flourish in those hot-beds of vice, the private gardens of England, none is more deep-rooted than the treasonable practice of stuffing the beds with ready-made plants (smuggled in, no doubt, in a warming-pan). This is known as 'planting' and is done by numberless Old Pretenders, in the evening, with the help of a trowel, a watering-can and numberless unnamed varieties of midges, gnats, bats, etc.

The lovable part of 'planting' is digging the little

Fig. xiv. Plantigrade War-dance.

holes in the ground and the difficult part is finding a clean bit of arm to rub your forehead with where the midges, bats, etc., have been biting it, digging treasonable little holes in it, etc.

"Water," say the Manuals, "should now be poured into the trowel-holes with sufficient velocity to create a slight froth." Like beer. "This, however, speedily disappears." Just like beer. So pour in more water, plug in ready-made plant and squeeze earth inwards and downwards with fists, thus causing muddy water to squirt outwards and upwards into face.

In consolidating soil finally round plant you have privilege, not often enjoyed by gardeners, of dancing plantigrade war-dance upwards and downwards in middle of valuable border. Make the most of this (see Fig. xiv), after which there will be nothing more to do except refrain from planting ready-made boots all over newly-made beds or wiping dirty face on clean trowel, etc.

WEED HOE !

(Plantain, etcetera.)

" One year's Seeding, seven years' weeding."
OLD SORE.

" The secret of weeding is never to begin."
CAPTAIN PONTOON.

In theory the most tedious occupation in the world, weeding in practice is a dangerous hysteria. It comes suddenly without warning. . . . You see a plantain here, a bindweed there . . . you stoop down. A little groundsel in the rose bed . . . you grab at it. A whorl of goose-grass among the asters . . . you're off !

Ground-ivy among the sweet-peas. Have at it ! *Cat's-whiskers* among the carrots, *Job's comforters* choking the phloxes, *leechwort* bleeding the dahlias to death ! Down on your knees, pulling, gouging, tearing, cursing ! Not a moment to lose.

An hour goes by, two hours, three hours, you haven't scratched the surface of it ! *Creeping-thistle* undermining the whole herbaceous border ! *Charlock, chick-weed, horse-tail, coltsfoot, pig-sporran !* Still pulling, still tearing, still swearing. Dinner-time. Grab a cutlet as if it were hemlock-and-two-vetch and hurl it into the fire-place. Dinner over. At it again, prising huge dandelions out of lawn by light of hurricane lantern.

Bed at last. But what a sleep ! Hands clutching, knees shaking, body writhing, brain reeling.

"*Calf's-tail !*" you bellow as nightmare grips you, ripping cord out of pyjama-waist. "*Crowsfoot !*" you mutter, poking yourself in the eye.

"*Joshua's beard !*" you jibber, lurching over in bed and tearing handfuls off husband's chin. "*Upsi-daisy !*" you prise the baby out of its cot and plunge it into the dirty-clothes basket.

"*Deadly-nightshade !*" With final shout of victory you wake up pouring with perspiration to find you have weeded the whole bedroom beyond repair. . . .

PRUNING

A. *Fruit Trees.*

There is never exactly the right amount of garden. You have to be either increasing it by sowing, mulching and grafting or decreasing it by thinning out, cutting back and, of course, Pruning.

Thinning out can safely be left to sparrows, slugs, wire-worms and (particularly in the case of sweet-peas) *mice*—though the latter tend to overdo it and it is perhaps worth recording the famous MacSicker or Ca'Canny method of sowing sweet-peas adopted by our friend Angus MacFungus, viz. first dip the seeds in paraffin and red lead (against mice) and then sow seeds six inches deep (in mouse-traps).

Pruning is easy, because the instructions are usually so lucid. For instance, " in pruning currant bushes it is a good rule to cut all new shoots off the old wood of *red*-currants to enable the new fruit to form on the old shoots, but to cut all *old* shoots off the *black*-currants to enable the stewed fruit to shoot off the *red*-currants " (and *vice versa*, or more lucidly, *tutti frutti*).

It is much the same with apple trees, but more difficult to explain, since there are no black apples.

B. *Roses.*

In pruning roses, also, we have a good guiding principle, viz. to promote strong shoots in weak growers and cut out weaker shoots in strong growers by *cutting back to the third dormant eye facing outwards in April*, except for special climbers that bloom on short shoots in July and, of course, shooters that climb in special long bloomers in August or utter bounders that shoot in climbing shorts in September—all of whom must be cut dead or, alternatively, *shot at sight*.

Much, however, depends on the species and on the purpose of cultivation : for general, as opposed to " show " purposes, *one dormant eye* has been found sufficient for Cleopatra (dark peach), Victor Hugo, and Countess Annesley, whereas those preferring a lighter treatment, such as Admiral Dewey (brick-red, suffused purple), Lady Godiva (blush), Madame D'Arblay and Dean Hole (lemon) may be pegged down and left with two to three dormant eyes facing upwards.

Note.—Captain Pontoon has just rung us up to say that for Dean Nuisance (pale flesh) and such hybrid twaddlers as Knatchbull Twee (fawny), he recommends pegging down firmly, removing all snags (bags, etc.), mulching well with road-scrapings and leaving with both eyes dormant and definitely face downwards.

WATERING

There are only two ways of watering (see moist pictures overleaf).

A FEW CUTTING REMARKS

' Striking and Layering ' or, if one might be intelligible for once, ' taking a cutting ', is nothing to do with potting-out, hitting-back, etc., with your old Scotch gardener in the greenhouse, or even with cutting a caper in the kitchen-garden, and the idea is to proceed as follows :

1. *Striking.* Cut a sprig of say, *Ampilopsis Madame*

Two common methods of watering.

Guillotine, at the twenty-third joint from the root, or somewhere ; strike cutting trenchantly into potful of rich compost ; next day, cutting dies of Nostalgia Jolly-naturalis and you are left with potful of rich compost. (The process can be repeated indefinitely, especially by jolly rich chap with potful of money.)

2. *Layering.* Push stem of *Amputopsis* (or whatever it is) right down flat on the ground—the wind or the dog will have done this already—and peg it there permanently with clothes-pegs or croquet-hoops. After a few days draw Fig. xv, which shows *new shoots springing up in dotted lines* (to indicate that new shoots will never be visible except in Fig. xv in dotted lines).

Fig. xv.

LOOKING ON THE WEEDICIDE

One of the more lovable perpetual labours is the purging of the garden by means of some widely advertised solution of weedicide, loamifact or wormideath, " *while avoiding* ", as the manual suggests, " *the indiscriminate use of highly concentrated arsenical compounds* " (Carried *nem. con.*).

" For attacking weeds," recommends Mrs. Love-death, the well-known weed-killer (amateur champion 1928, '29, '33 and '35), " a *fair* day should be chosen, neither too hot nor too cold, not a morning after heavy rain, but a day slightly overcast with likelihood of rain to follow."

Visibility, we can only add, should be moderate, Channel roughish, with no prospect of cold dry heat or pelting equatorial droughts to follow. Above all, not a *foul* day, with visibility nil, sick headache and likelihood of boiled mutton with tapioca pudding to follow.

Very well then : having chosen a day of fair promise, select a plant of foul aspect which you feel quite certain is a weed. Stab it with weedicide, probe and inject deadly solution. Come back three days later and try to figure out why plant has burst into bloom as a riot of *Auricula Floribunda*.

MOWING AND ROLLING

I. *Mopping and Mowing.*

This perspirational labour can be done either with a hand-mower, in which case the only real difficulty is to persuade anyone who has ever done it before to do it again, or with a motor-mower, in which case the difficulty is to stop everyone who has never done it before having a cut at it at once.

Hand-mowing consists of (*a*) *non-stop mowing*, which is when the knives are " set too kind " and the machine canters kindly over the greensward without affecting the length of the grass one way or the other, or (*b*) *full-stop mowing*, which is when the knives are " set too cruel " and the machine suddenly jibs, gnashing its teeth madly into the turf while the handle socks you a cruel punch in the solar plexus.

Motor-mowing, on the other hand, usually turns out to be either (*a*) *non-stop motoring*, or (*b*) *non-start mowing*; because the kick-starter is always more likely to start kicking than to start the motor, whereas if you do manage to get it started the motor-mower is like the plough—once you have put your hand to it you must *never look back*, or you may find yourself motoring

down the gravel path (Crumbs !) or mowing your way slap through the whole garden-city and out on to the by-pass (Crikey ! that's hell, that was . . .).

II. *Love's Labour's Lost.*

Sooner or later you will have to buy a *Roller* since even a warranted non-jibbing jobbing gardener will jib at bringing his own roller, particularly if you live at the top of a long steep hill.

What's more, you will have to learn to love the extraordinary Clonksqueelungular noise to which all garden-rollers give tongue when in full-cry, because it is frightfully dangerous to try conclusions with the Noise by getting inside the roller and attempting to oil the tongue (*see frightful Clonksqueelungular conclusion drawn by artist below*).

Not that you will be doing much of this kind of labour, anyway: as everyone knows, it is useless to roll the lawn in *dry* weather and, since damp wormcasts when rolled flat suffocate the grass (though not, alas, the worms underneath), it is equally useless to roll the lawn in *wet* weather.

(*Logical but unclonksqueelungular conclusion, drawn by Capt. Pontoon:* It is useless to Roll the Lawn.)

SPIT THE TENTH

POSSIBLE GARDENING

A garden is a loathsome thing—so what?
CAPT. W. D. PONTOON.

WELL, there it all is—on paper. Or most of it—because as a matter of fact there are about A Thousand and One Lovable Doings and Don'tings for Garden Zealots which we hadn't the heart or the time to mention.

This *time factor* is serious. As the Garden Books say " a little experience will speedily convince you " that there are (alas) only 52 week-ends, a fortnight's holiday and a few fine summer evenings for carrying out all this Plotting and Planning, Earth-control, Ding-worship and other Manurial Rites ; this Sowing and Mowing and Grubbing up the weeds and weeding out the grubs ; and all that grafting and grousing and binding and boasting and pegging down and forking in and stumping up ; and eke, withal, mayhap and (peradventure) *Alack*, perpetually damning-back the Dank encroachments of your Unpleasaunce.

So what ?

We'll tell you what. *There are only two systems for working it*, we mean for working it so that you have time to Love your Garden and yet turn up at the office (with or without your green fingers) frequently

Mr. X. was always a keen gardener.

enough to hold down your job, and keep off the dole.
The two systems are *Dumb Gardening* and *Wildflower
Gardening*.

*　　　*　　　*

Dumb Gardening is when you keep your nose glued
to the grindstone (not the one in the Unpleasaunce)
till you've got a cool unctuous £5000 a year and can
delegate the whole snobgoblinatious garden nuisance
to a lovable head-gardener (*not* Angus MacFungus)
and his seven earth-bound assistants, while *you* sit
about and *don't do anything* but just keep on loving
in the same old way, and explaining (at the office) that
everything's lovely in the garden and that you've
always been a keen gardener yourself. . . .

*　　　*　　　*

Wildflower Gardening is simpler still, because all
you have to do to be a Wildflower Gardener is to
amble out every week-end with a stick and a dog and
note with Approval, or in a bad season with Contempt,
the rather ramshackle results of Dame Nature's
endeavours to do a bit of gardening on her own without
reference to the Impossible Manuals.

(The stick, by the way, is for improving your golf
by striking off the heads of any wildflowers which look
as if they needed cutting-back, and the dog is for
running wild after the Distant Prospect of a Rabbit,
rolling in decomposed carcases, barking (inspired by
the Distant Prospect of a Cow), getting mulched up to
the eyes in clay-soil, leaf-mould, etc., and having to be

given water, weeded-out, raked-over, decomposed, fumigated, and forced into its basket when you get home again.)

THIRD BUMP

BEYOND THE UNPLEASAUNCE

BEE-KEEPING UNVEILED

How do you doth ? (Correct greeting for bees.)

I. AREN'T BEES SWEET ?

HOW *doth* the little buzzy bee improve each shining hour ? Frankly, we don't know : but considering how often it has been held up as an example (see Fig. i. overleaf) the Bee is a surprisingly popular little contraption.

Everyone seems to like the Bee, in spite of the fact that you can't *pat it*, or *put your shirt on it*, or *breed it for the Show ring*, or even *shoot it* in September on the moors.

Military men, for instance, admire its heroism in battle, since they know that a bee commits *hara-kiri* every time it bayonets you with its little sting. (All the same, on finding one crawling up his trouser-leg, even a V.C. might wish to remind the little Samurai that a good soldier never throws his life away unnecessarily.)

Fig. 1. . . . held up as an example . . .

Socialists wax lyrical about the way the bees have organized themselves on trades union lines, the little sewing-bees getting on with their sewing, and the little spelling-bees getting on with their matric (Certificate B only, of course) and none of them ever dreaming of doing anything but pursue their registered occupations. . . .

Indeed, politicians of all colours are reassured to find that there is a recognized class of (male) bees, called Drones, who are not expected to do anything in life but keep up a monotonous and probably meaningless booming noise.

Even the Drones are cherished by those for whom Ro-mance is Everything, because once a year the Queen Bee leads them a dance into the stratosphere where the Strongest Flier of Them All becomes Her Airman Lover (and dies immediately of exhaustion, while the rest die of disappointment).

Our own conscientious Queens have, of course, always respected the Queen-Bee for being, literally, the Mother of her People ; and as a matter of fact all women think bees are rather sweet (something in that, too) though they really like bumble-bees best, and nine out of ten women (the thing is almost unmentionable) secretly long to stroke the handsome beast on its furry little bumble-beehind.

Bee Prepared.

II. BEE-KEEPING UNVEILED

A person who keeps *Bees* is called an *Apiarist*. On the other hand, a person who keeps *Apes* is *not* called a *Beepiarist*.

(This is just as unfair as the fact that a person who clips *trees* into *shapes* is called a *Topiarist*, whereas a person who clips *topes* into *shapes*, or vice versa, is *not* called a *Treepiarist*.)

The only real difficulty however about Bee-keeping is, of course, *to keep the bee*.

Bees are fairly easy to catch, because every now and then they get fed up with their futilitarian state and suddenly form swarms (right ! quick march !) and buzz off vaguely on a Crusade.

Now is your chance ! Put on a black-speckled boater and camouflage your face in butter-muslin. Any conscientious bee, seeing that you have not only taken the veil but borrowed the vicar's hat as well, will conclude that you are Peter the Hermit or St. Bee, or some other heaven-sent Leader, and will follow you blindly into the nearest bee-hive.

So far so good.　Having got your bee, and made sure that it is a genuine mellifluous one, or sweet-bee, and not just a baby bumble-bee, or bumble-puppy, the

. . . taken the veil . . .

next step is to get it back into a utilitarian, or skeptical state of mind and so prevent it buzzing off again on a Second Crusade.

Nowadays, this problem is particularly difficult, chiefly because bees are no longer content with the old-fashioned thatched bee-cosies made of straw: to the modern educated bee these dome-like structures suggest St. Paul's Cathedral or Santa Sophia, so that she gets religious mania and goes zooming off again In Search of The Vicar.

So the only thing to do is to provide your bees with a little white villa fitted with gables and wax floors, and to prevent the female workers from giving notice by offering vacuum-cleaners, own wireless, electric fire in bedroom, two afternoons and evenings a week, cap and apron optional, and no nonsense about bee-ing in by ten o'clock.

The only other thing you must do is to give them plenty to eat in the winter to make up for their honey-reserves which you have taken away from them in the summer.   Coarse molasses will do—but we warn you, the thing they like best is, naturally, *Honey*.   You can get it quite cheap at the Grocer's.   All you have to do now is to wait patiently till summer and then *Press Button Bee and Get Your Honey Back.*

*   *   *

A NOTE ON THE BEE IN POESY AND MYTH

By Captain Pontoon, M.C., R.E., retd.

The scientific truth about bees is as unpleasant as the classical references to them are inaccurate.   The hive is a highly mechanized unit and the bee is an entirely unsuitable subject for romantic affection or any sort of poetical affectation.

Consider the crude but economical process by which honey is made.   The bee sucks it from the flower and deposits it in a special stomach from which it subsquently sicks it up into a cell or vomitorium, or, alternatively, retains it for twenty-four hours and then sweats it out into its waistcoat pockets in the form of beeswax.

Another proof that the bee is practical rather than poetical is the way it feeds its young on breadcrumbs and other vegetable debris which it brushes out of the fur on its stomach.

Is it to be supposed that you could win the friendship of a creature of this kind, as the Latin poet Vergil suggests, by "*planting crocuses and erecting a statue to Priapus*"?

The rest of Vergil's information is equally hysterical. *They sharpen their stings*, he tells us, *on their beaks, and do not breed like other animals but 'find' their eggs.* (One can only conclude that somebody had been trying to explain to him about the Cuckoo.)

In another passage he states that, since bees cannot swim (agreed), it is essential to *place stepping-stones for them in all the neighbouring streams.* The most charitable explanation is that this is an interpolation from another poem which Vergil was writing, simultaneously, about *slugs*.

It is not surprising that at this stage the poet, feeling that he was making an utter fool of himself, suddenly abandoned the subject of bees and decided to finish the poem (Georgics IV) by telling the rather more probable story of how Orpheus went to hell for Eurydice.

Indeed there is only one point on which it is possible to agree whole-heartedly with Vergil. "Do not," he advises, "burn crabs near the hive." One might go even further and say, "*Don't burn crabs at all, anywhere.*"

Similarly deluded notions are found amongst ancient philosophers and mystics. Aristotle, for instance, announces that bees are "divinely inspired" and adds (whether as evidence of this or not is uncertain) that "they carry pebbles for ballast against storms". While Mahomet actually admits this soulless insect to Paradise; and the Ancient Priestesses of Ceres went so far as to believe that the *Moon* was a Bee.

It is a relief to turn from such ravings to the very

reasonable doubts expressed by Hamlet (see Fig. ii), or even to the romantic but, after all, harmless infatuation of the poet Browning's Ode to Bee in England. . . .

> [*Editors*—" Are you sure you're being quite accurate yourself ? "
> *Captain P.*—" Bumbledom to you, gentlemen ! "]

Fig. ii.

A BRIEF REPORT

UPON

THE MENTAL CONDITION OF THE HEN

(Compiled at the request of the Royal Poultricultural Society)

by

Commendatore-Bombaduce Coccaloria, Professor of Eggalomania, University of Leghorn,[1]

and

Genl. Sir Geo. Buff-Orpington, K.C.S.I., Hon. Egg-Watcher to H.H. The Sultan of Barndore.

I. SUMMARY

THE very high incidence of hen-hatred in all rural districts obliges us to record, in self-defence, that desire for truth is the sole reason for the pessimistic nature of this report.

We regret, therefore, to find that the characteristic mental condition of the Common or Barndoor Fowl (*Gallina non compos mentis*) is the confused attitude commonly known (among hens) as *Schizophrenia* or Split Personality, resulting, as everyone knows, in total inability to make decisions of any kind, or answer the simplest conundrums such as (*a*) Which came first, the hen or the egg ? (The answer is, of course, in the neggative) or (*b*) Why does a chicken (try to) cross the road ? (The answer is, of course, *to get to Heaven out of it.*)

[1] Inventor of the Fascist system of inoculating hens with spirit of *Sacro eggoismo*.

Strange and indeed sad as it may seem, in all the feathered world the only creature which is never cocksure is (alas) The Hen.

As Linnæus, scholar and naturalist, observes:

Unable to make up its mind.

"*Hennus non potest de aliquo superficere mentem.*" (The Hen is unable to make up its mind about anything.)

On the contrary it scratches its head about everything—*with its feet* (which it erroneously believes to be the correct method) and goes about *gaping.*

As the famous Franciscan, St. Faverolle Incubator, laments :

"*Ecce! caput gratinat pede se infeliciter Hennus.*"

(Lo! Haplessly the Hen scratches itself on the head by means of the foot.)

This fatal indecision of the Hen manifests itself in countless ways, of which we now propose to give (alas) countless examples.

II. DEFECTIVE EGG-RHYTHM

Instead of laying its eggs in the spring the Hen attempts to lay all the year round. No other bird does this.

The reason is probably as follows :

(i) The Hen, as all unprejudiced poultrographers admit, was invented by the Ancient Chinese, about the same time that they invented printing and the mariner's compass. It is now considered doubtful whether the Chinese originally conceived of all these inventions as Utilities or as implements of torture, but it is known that they gave the bird the name ' *Ho-Heng* ' (lit.: " Winged bagpipe causing maximum distress to philosophers ").

(ii) First introduced into Europe by the Romans, the Hen was thrown across all the principal rivers of France by Julius Cæsar and finally flown across the English Channel by mistake, or blown across possibly by thunder-storms.

(iii) During these prolonged compulsory migrations the Hen became irrevocably confused about everything, including the seasons of the year ; and was thereafter quite unable to make up its mind when, and particularly when not, to lay its eggs.

(iv) Consequently it took to laying as frequently as possible in the hope that at least some of the eggs would be laid in the spring.

*   *   *

Worse still, the modern poultry-farmer lays himself out to heighten the Hen's geographical incertitude—deliberately astounding the bird by shining lights in its face after it has gone to bed (in imitation of the midnight sun, Aurora Borealis, etc.)—and thus reduces it to a state of Schizophrantic Despair in which it produces eggs, fresh eggs, newlaid eggs, homelaid eggs, and even imported national mark eggs, not only all the year round but all day long as well—and sometimes even in the middle of the night—its psychology being now irremediably egg-centric.

III.   CONNUBIAL INDECISION

Mental confusion, one would think, could go no further. One would be wrong. There are some hens which are confused even as to their own sex, and have therefore felt themselves compelled to adopt a feathery form of the epicene garment known as Oxford bags.

This vagueness among hens as to whether they are male or female is, however, mainly due to their fear that they can lay eggs whether they are married or not—a confusion which is shared by everyone except, of course, the cock, who doesn't care tuppence about finicking distinctions of this sort and has consequently been adopted by the French as their national emblem.

IV. PSYCHOLOGY OF HEN-FLIGHT

Close students of Hen-life have noted that the Hen when pursued becomes dynamically distraught, i.e. flies cock-eyed ; viz. after taxi-ing madly down the hen-run it almost invariably makes a forced landing

on its chest without ever (alas) having risen from the ground.

No other bird does this, and the thing has hitherto remained a complete henigma, since the fowl, though dimly aware of the hexplanation, is for some reason unable to make a clean breast of it.

The truth is of course quite simple. Its egg-rhythm being as explained above hopelessly jazzed-up, the Hen, unlike other birds, has *no time* for flying and feels compelled to alight precipitately—even before it has risen from the ground—*in case it should be time to lay some more eggs.*

V. ABORTIVE MIGRATORY IMPULSE, NOSTALGIA, ETC.

The practice of standing on top of the coop and beating the air fruitlessly with both wings is believed by most people to be an attempt on the part of the hen to cool the ovifactory mechanism, or egg-bearings, which, as is well known, become overheated when a rate of eggpulsion of over a hundred eggs per minute is attempted.

This is wrong. The hen is not fanning itself.

Coop-flapping, accompanied usually by cluckular utterance (flap-doodle), is a *nostalgic* manœuvre designed to give the bird the feeling that it is on the point of migrating—preferably to China.

Actually the Hen is, of course, aware that it dare not migrate more than a few yards owing to the risk of showering eggs indiscriminately over open towns (unprovided with pullet-proof shelters) thus laying itself open to counter shell-fire, etc.

*   *   *

Similarly, hens are often to be observed travelling about the country in hampers by slow passenger-train, and this also gives rise to wrong ideas.

These hen-excursions are not due to any conscious desire of the poultry-keeper to defy the rule against putting all one's eggs in one basket (by stuffing all his hens into one packing-case). Nor is hen-hampering a manifestation of active cruelty on the part of organized hen-haters.

The simple explanation is that the hens are sub-consciously trying to migrate without actually leaving the ground. . . .

Owing to their bemused state of mind they keep getting into the wrong trains, so that by the time they reach a terminus they are very glad to be let out again, though naturally disappointed to find that they have not yet reached China.

Furthermore, to quote Professor H. du Guizzard Wyandotte, D.Hen. (Zillebeke), whose henmanship is unquestioned, " it is surely a suppressed racial memory of their Eastern origin which compels so many hens to subconsciously lay China eggs in their sleep ".

VI. THE VOCAL POINT

It is generally agreed that Hens cannot *sing*, and that the nearest they get to it, namely the loud ovopæan or triumphal egg-solo, is (alas) more in the nature of a College yell than an anthem. A much mooter point is whether the Hen can *talk*. Many amateur Hen-watchers have spent fruitless hours listening to its querulous mutterings in the hope that, like the parrot, it would suddenly start making vulgar observations.

The truth is that no Hen has ever got further than clearing its throat because, though they undoubtedly *want* to talk, Hens have never been able to make up their minds what their first remark ought to be. They are also embarrassed, possibly, by the suspicion that since nobody nowadays understands old Chinese their comments might be totally ignored, even by the Poultry Gazette.

VII. MENTAL CONDITION OF THE POULTRY-FARMER

It is hoped that this report, by explaining, and perhaps arousing sympathy with, the pathological impulses of the Hen may tend to elucidate at the same time some of the pathological impulses of the Poultry-farmer. Of these, the most conscious is (alas) his impulse to collect all the eggs he can find and throw

them one by one at the nearest Hen; but more dangerous is his tendency to *identify himself subconsciously with his poultry*, thus falling into such habits as scratching the head with the foot, taxi-ing madly down the garden path and landing on the wishbone, and even standing on the roof and flapping his arms in a state of frenzied indecision as to whether he oughtn't to migrate to China and have done with it. . . .

[The Editors regret that they are unable to print the rest of this invaluable Report, which proved to be rather longer than they anticipated. Copies are available, however (Crown 8vo, Egg-bound, 266 pp.), for interested readers. Applications should be accompanied by stamped addressed envelope and cheque for £266–0–0 ; payment in eggs will not be accepted.]

FOURTH BUMP

THE WIND-ON-THE-HEATH BOTHER

A KHAKI STUDY FOR CAMPERS, TRAMPERS AND EMPIRE-SAVERS

THE WIND-ON-THE-HEATH BOTHER

. . . bread I dropped in the river.
This is the life for a man like me. . . .

THE ROADSIDE LIAR.

The Brotherhood of the Road.

I. LOOKING FOR ENGLAND

A SHORT while ago newspaper readers awoke to a new scare, a new terror of the country-side, in a word—*Leatherjackets.*

What were they ? Insects ? Fungi ? Fascists ? No one seemed to know, but everyone agreed that (like the Dardanelles [1]) they were multiplying rapidly and were becoming a pest, almost a plague. . . .

The motorists soon supplied the answer. Swarms of these vermin, they declared, could be observed every week-end, waddling and wobbling all over our great arterial speedways—a menace to the Human Race.

The Human Race.

" The upper-body, or thorax, of the typical specimen," stated the Editor of the *The Road Hog Breeder* in a powerful article, " is invariably *brown*, special markings being confined to the legs which are usually striped yellow-and-black. . . ."

The female pest being indistinguishable from the male, nothing short of a mass-drive of 100-m.p.h. steam-rollers, declared the Editor, would serve to stem the appalling rate of increase of these blights.

[1] According to Mr. Milton Hayes, the well-known expert on things in general.

Meanwhile we have a rather daring idea of our own that the Leatherjackets might (eventually) be re-categorized as *people* (and taxed by the Chancellor of the Exchequer for attempting to enjoy themselves).

The Leatherjackets.

There is something rather human in the way they set out every week-end from London and Manchester and anywhere else where they can't be happy (especially on Sunday) in search of something which, alas, no longer exists. . . .

In search of England.

II. LOOKING FOR TROUBLE

Unlike the miserable Leatherjackets, however, there are numerous inhabitants of these Isles who have comfortable homes and are hardly unhappy at all. This, they know instinctively, is Wrong (and in ex-

In search of discomfort.

treme cases, Sin). So once a year they feel obliged to drive themselves ruthlessly out into the small open spaces *in search of discomfort*.

Their practical object is, of course, to avert the Decline and Fall of the British Empire by hurting themselves as much as possible with palliasses, billicans, canvas-buckets, bits of string, etc.

As everyone knows, there are two recognized ways of averting the Decline, namely (*a*) Caravanning and (*b*) Tent-pegging, the history and theory of which are as follows :

(*a*)

The Caravan Method of making life completely inconvenient was really discovered by the stupendous pioneer Mr. Cecil B. de Mille of Hollywood, N.J., who invented caravans (and called them ' Covered Wagons ', so that Americans would get the idea) and went gold-rushing all over the Socony mountains from Alberta to Bloemfontein in search of Major Douglas.

The object of the Caravan Method is to cover as much territory as possible before you get scalped, and it works even better now than it used to because with a caravan behind it you can't reverse your automobile, so if you miss a turning you may easily have to circumcaravanavigate the Globe. . . .

(*N.B.* The door is smallish and sooner or later you do scalp yourself.)

(*b*)

The Tent Method was introduced by General Lord Baden-Powell (who suffered brilliant hardships on the African Bushveldt, the Canadian Rockies, the Mound

at Lord's Cricket Ground and other exceptionally
unyielding places) and is therefore much more British,
uncomfortable, unwaterproof, etc.

Morally, on the other hand, it has the weakness that
whereas with a caravan you cannot avoid sleeping in
the thing in all weathers, with a tent you *can* avoid
trying to pitch the rudyard thing in a thunderstorm
by going to an hotel for the night—thus letting down
the Empire.

Straight campers, however, invariably go right ahead
regardless of wind or rain, thus keeping the Flag
flying, letting down the tent, etc.

Keeping the tent flying.

But whichever method the comfortable classes select
they have the same opportunities of immolating themselves upon the horns of the camp-bed or mortifying
the flesh with white-hot enamel mugs, or flinging their

bodies into icy rivers before breakfast for King and Country.

We have no space to describe all the routine instruments of Camp-torture and have therefore chosen one of the very latest of which we have recently received from abroad the following remarkable details, and which we recommend to all camp-scarred veterans in search of a new sensation. . . .

The 'Alsbald' [1] Concentrated Hungarian Camping Stove
(Spit out all contrafiction!)
§ *General-Detail*

Like all the good campingstove the Alsbald Stove

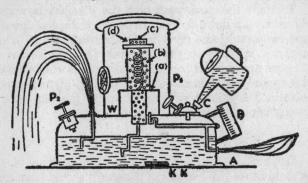

The Alsbald Stove.

are *highly inflammable* and when ignited burns with a strong orange-coloured flame which *can never be igstinguished*.

The Alsbald Stoves is fabricated only by the Alsbald Coy. at Mpsyszl, Benzolvania (N.W.Hungaria), condemned

[1] From the high German diplomatic word 'alsbald'—lit.: 'forthwith' or alternatively 'soon'.

misdemeanors only being employed in the fabrication due to the extreme danger of work.

The Alsbald Stove has not been patented in many countries as it has been found unnecessary for many reasons.

§ *Working advices*
(Follow closefully !)

To fill the stove insert the special fuel can the special fuel can then be pumped into the All-Weather filling-cap (C) the fuel can then be pumped out of the fuel can then by motions of the plunger (Pi) the pressures inside the stove must be maintained at 15° (Tzentipede) owing to the small plunger (Pii) on the opposite side without which the fuel will tzentrifrugally lose itself out of the Emergency-Hole (E), *see upwards*, which cannot be avoided.

To ignite the stove work both the Plungers in reverse directions (i.e. downwards and upwards instead of upwards and downwards) also revolving the knurled knob (Ki), and applying sulphurs to the smallhole (X) (not shown on diagram upwards but perfectly detectable as when sulphurs are applied to the smallholes (a), (b), (c), (d) and (e) the Alsbald Stove must explode forthwith (alsbald) with a strong orange-colour bomb-sound).

§ *Small Adjustings*

Dampnis is destructive to the good working of the Alsbald Stove. When jets of flames (jj) should issue from the Safety-Hole (A) just underneath the Hand-gripps (B) this must be dew to the storms having penetrated the All-Weather filling-cap (See ?). Remedy ; unscrew the gnarled gnob (G) in tzentre of underneath and lose the fuel out, dense smoke-fumes issuing from all parts of the Alsbald Stove proves that the flame is igstinguished and all is soon (alsbald) in good order again.

§ *Warning !*

The Alsbald Stove ignites only with the special High-inflammation benzin-fuel obtainable only from the Alsbald Coy. of Mpsyszl, Benzolvania (N.W.Hungaria), attempting to use all other fuels will only oblige the stove to explode itself with strongest orange-colour fulminations Obtainable only from the Alsbald Coy. of Mpsyszl, Benzolvania (N.W.Hungaria) which is not responsible.

(SPIT OUT ALL CONTRAFICTION)

—Advt.

III.   RALLY-HO

But the Empire's most valuable assets are, as everybody knows, our Wonderful Boy Scouts and our Implacable Girl Guides. Consequently it is worth making an effort to appreciate what these young assets get up to in the Great Open Air and, if possible, what they mean by it.

Flag-wagging, Codes, etc.

One of the first things all Scouts and Guides have to learn is the right side and the wrong side of the Union

Jack : this enables them not only to keep the Flag flying, but to keep it flying the right way up. It also prevents any tendency to fly it inside-out, which, as everyone knows, is the Signal of Distress.

Thus whenever a Girl Guide discovers a Desert Island she can, without showing any signs of distress, annexe it properly for England, and it will always be shown on the map in red, the right way up, and she will get her *Keen Observer's Badge* and will probably wear it inside out, bless her !

*   *   *

Another very clever trick is the use by the Scout (or Guide) of Codes and Signals—the chief Codes being the Morse Code, the Deaf and Dumb Alphabet, the Scout's Code of Honour, and the Semaphore (Girl Guides, Pinaphore) Alphabet.

Many a Girl Güide has *saved India*, again and again, by being able to signal the first verse of the national anthem (again and again) to a deaf-and-dumb Staff Officer.

*   *   *

Similarly, every Scout learns to ' lay a trail ' which prevents enemies of the Empire finding out which way he has gone.

The following are some of the secret signs in common use among Scouts, Tramps, Hitler Youths, Duce-bambinos, and dope-traffickers, all over the world :

Signs of Coming and Going

1. ⟶ =I have gone this way.

2. ⟵ =Now I come back again disaway, yesno ? huh ?

3. =I have gone to sleep for 3 days.

4. =I have gone { mad. off the map. }

5. =I have gone nudist and given my clothes to this cow.

Besides drawing these signs in the dust on the backs of motor-cars, cows, etc., the Scout has, of course, innumerable other ways of disguising his whereabouts, indicating his honourable intentions and so on, such as knotting blades of grass together and bending them horizontally to see which direction he is going in, splicing fir-trees together vertically and bending them to his will and so on.

Signs of Hiding and Seeking

1. ⑤ ↗ = I am hiding five paces from here.

2. 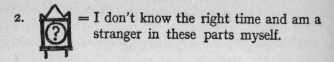 = I don't know the right time and am a stranger in these parts myself.

3. !⑥! = I have found sixpence.

4. E ⑦ S = I have lost my bearings.

5. ? ⚹ ? = I have lost my braces.

6.  = I have lost my memory and my t e m p e r and given m y s e l f up to the Police.

Code of Honour

The Scouts' Code of Honour is simple, empirical and totally jamborical : he is kind to his King, his patrol-leader, his employer, and sometimes even to his father and mother, *no matter what class he thinks they belong to :* he is loyal to all animals, vegetables, etc., including Girl-guides, Scoutmistresses, and even women police-men : he has loyal knees : he is pure in thought and word and behind the ears : he is thrifty, nosey, posey, and *always prepared* (for something which will never happen) : he smiles and whistles (alas) simultaneously

under all difficulties (and probably even under water) :
he worships the Open Air life and is therefore biggish,
priggish, etc., and, in shorts, almost a (country)
gentleman.

The whole thing has been summed up (alas) mnemoni-
cally by Dean Nuisance, who has been responsible for
innumerable Camp-fire Yawns, Damp-fire Dotties, etc.,
in an easily remembered saga or songaree. . . .

Dean Nuisance's Poem.

" Scout Glory "

Loyal, brave, thrifty :
Pure in thought and behind the cheerful knees.
Prepared to interfere obediently,
Whistles kindly under water.

Of course, the whole affair is, admittedly, rather
militaristic. Only the other day a Nazi schoolboy
visiting London said to us " Yes, we also have Boyscouts in Germany but also our Boyscouts are a not-
military organization not like your Boyscouts who are
always prepared."

It is true. One cannot conceal it. The only question
is, what are they prepared for ?

And the only answer is (German Patrol-Führers
please note)—*for the Boer War*.

Spoor War

Owing to the large numbers of animals in the British
Empire which may not all be entirely loyal, every
Scout is taught how to *Spoor*, so that he will be able
to track down the animal to its lair, and, if necessary,
prod it into a more loyal frame of mind with his pole.

The same thing is, of course, often done in the case of a disloyal tramp.

Spooring is not easy. In the first place one requires a large amount of clean snow or virgin mud for the animals to make their footmarks in, and this

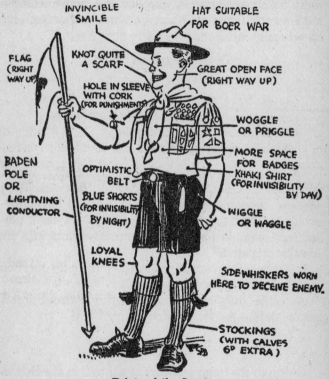

INVINCIBLE SMILE

HAT SUITABLE FOR BOER WAR

FLAG (RIGHT WAY UP)

KNOT QUITE A SCARF

GREAT OPEN FACE (RIGHT WAY UP)

HOLE IN SLEEVE WITH CORK (FOR PUNISHMENT)

WOGGLE OR PRIGGLE

MORE SPACE FOR BADGES

BADEN POLE OR LIGHTNING CONDUCTOR

OPTIMISTIC BELT

KHAKI SHIRT (FOR INVISIBILITY BY DAY)

BLUE SHORTS (FOR INVISIBILITY BY NIGHT)

WIGGLE OR WAGGLE

LOYAL KNEES

SIDE WHISKERS WORN HERE TO DECEIVE ENEMY.

STOCKINGS (WITH CALVES 6ᴰ EXTRA)

Points of the Scout.

is not always available. When the ground is hard the footprints are invisible and it becomes necessary to lay down enormous stretches of plasticine in front of the animal which is subsequently to be tracked, and this is always very expensive.

It would be tedious to list all the spoors of all the animals, criminals, and casuals in the British Empire that a Boy Scout might have to prod; a few of those most commonly found in England will suffice to show both the fascination and the vital importance of spooring.

Spoors

1. Pheasant of doubtful loyalty going in two directions at once.

2. Mongoose standing on one leg, (or possibly five of clubs).

3. Ear-mark of Red Indian listening for approach of Guide Mistress.

4. Horse going lame, (or possibly going mad).

5. Horse standing still (problem: w h e r e   i s   t h e horse?)

6. Duck-billed platypus, (or possibly two ducks in single file).

If at the end of a long trail the animal proves to be loyal after all, the Scout will often find it possible to do the animal a good turn.

This is, of course, usually done by means of the Boy Scouts' special Good Turn Knife (see below). For example, it is a good turn to take a stone out of a horse's hoof, and similarly one can use the Knife for scraping barnacles or bus-tickets out of a badger's ear or any other place where disloyal debris might cause unnecessary suffering or imperil The Constitution.

The Loyal Knife.

(Showing some of its extra special fittings.)

1. The Sea Scout's stand-by, for taking wind out of enemy's sails.
2. For pulling chestnuts out of the fire or caramels out of horses' teeth.
3. For getting fly out of ointment, probing mysteries of universe, etc.
4. For taking needle out of haystack or last straw out of eye of camel.
5. For taking appendix out of loyal goat.
6. For extracting poisoned arrows from bicycle tyres, or last trump out of camel's kneedle.
7. For delving into past, dragging skeleton out of cupboard, etc.
8. For extracting subscriptions from sporrans.

Tips for Tenderfoots

How to choose a camping-site. (i) Find a quiet spot, easily accessible, on flat grassy ground, on a dry hillside near running water, open to the sun and well protected from the prevailing winds from all quarters. (ii) Establish by enquiry that all camping has been prohibited by the local Council in the interests of the Boarding-houses, or of the national death-rate. (iii) Go on whistling and shouting simultaneously and thanking heaven you are an Englishman, and find another place, on the edge of a cliff, open to the wind from all quarters, or on the slope of a sunless quagmire, where camping is permitted on payment of 10/– a sq. ft. (iv) Do not lose your temper and strike the tent, or curse the flies, or annoy the farmer by bathing in the cattle-trough or whistling and singing under water, or enjoying yourself in any way—there's never any need to behave like a savage—but roll your tent up neatly and pitch it over the cliff. . . .

How to tell the time by the sun. Point your watch at the sun, having previously set it (the watch) at half-past twelve or any suitable time. Now bisect the angle between twelve and, say, half-past five and wait five minutes. Point the watch at yourself and put the hands back five minutes ; this is, approximately, the time to put the watch back in your pocket.

How to tell which way the wind is blowing. Wet your whistle and hold up one finger in the air and keep your eye on the weathercock.

Time-table for Saturday camp.

3.30   Due at camping-ground.

4.30   If already at camping-ground, prepare refuse pits, hole for dirty-water and kitchen. (Hole for d.w. should be covered with ferns, etc., so that all the party can fall into it, in turns, etc.)

5.0	Tea.
5.30	Tea (not ready yet).
6.0	Tea (clearing up, falling into grease trap, etc.).
6.30	Pitch tent correctly.
7.30	Pitch voice correctly for camp-fire ditty.
8.30	Pitch darkness (light hurricane-lamp). Fix tent-flap.
9.30	Hurricane. Tent flaps. (light rainfall.)
10.30	Cloud-burst. Rush out into darkness, into refuse-pit, etc., and tighten guy-ropes in case tent-flops.
11.30	Hurricane has got inside hurricane-lamp and someone has mistaken your toe for a tent-peg and hammered it into the grease-trap.
12.30	Earthquakes, Forest Fires, Typhoons, Tidal Waves, etc.
12.31	Tent flops.
12.32	Whistling, singing, etc., under canvas. . . .
12.35	Strike camp if not already struck by lightning. . . .

Badges and Punishments

There seems to be a good deal of vagueness among civilian campers as to whether the innumerable little *badges* with which patrol-leaders spray themselves are all Decorations for Good Deeds, or whether some of them are not Endorsements of some kind proving that the scout has been punished for failing to make a Turk's Head Woggle, or driving a patrol-waggon to

The punishments.

the danger of the Empire while under the influence of cocoa.

Such people only show their ignorance of the spirit of Scoutship. Needless to say, there has never been a single case of a Boy Scout being drunk in charge of a tent-peg or attempting to boil a billican in a disloyal way or trying to score a good deed by giving the canary to the cat : the badges are all for officially checked feats of super-scoutcraft (such as lighting a match with only one box) ; the punishments are gratuitously inflicted, at the request of scouts who wish to harden their souls or purify their knees, for theoretical Bad Deeds such as saying " I hate you, I hate you ! " to the grease-trap. . . .

The punishments consist almost entirely of pouring different things such as cups of cold tea, tins of condensed milk, or buckets of warm motor-oil, into the various orifices in the scout uniform (see purifying picture, page 123).

§ *Appendix*

POINTS OF THE SKITE

THE Complete Opposite to a Scout, or to any loyal outdoor person with a Great Open Face, is the sort of youth whose behaviour fully entitles him (alas) to be called *A SKITE.* Let us run over his bad points (he has no good ones) just for the pleasure of those of us who feel qu.te certain we are all right.

A skite is always down at heel, down at the Pub and generally up to no good.

He smokes cheap advertized cigarettes and in general apes the man instead of manning the pumps.

He has no idea what time it is, except opening-time, or from which direction the wind is blowing and is always ready to stand another slacker a drink.

He has disloyal knees.

Instead of reading ' Scouting for Boys ', he goes out scouting for girls.

He bets on the Derby and goes to the dogs punctually every Saturday.

If he did a good deed he would forget to note it down in his diary, and if his uncle gave him £5 he would probably go right out and spend it !

He is ungrateful to his employer, thinks nothing of asking for a rise, and when curtly refused gets annoyed instead of going out smiling and whistling simultaneously.

He refuses to fight for King and Country, except (alas) in time of war. . . .

In short, he is an absolute Skite—*Up, lads, and pour a gallon of castor-oil down his disloyal throat.*

* * *

MORE TOP HUMOUR IN MAGNUM BOOKS AND METHUEN PAPERBACKS

W. C. Sellar & R. J. Yeatman
1066 AND ALL THAT

A book that has itself become part of our history. The authors made the claim that 'All the History you can remember is in the Book'—and for most of us, they were probably right. But it is their own unique interpretation of events which has made the book a classic; the result is an uproarious satire upon textbook history and our confused recollections of it.

AND NOW ALL THIS

In *1066 and all That* Messrs Sellar and Yeatman set out to provide a history book to end all history books—and succeeded brilliantly. In this hilarious sequel they turn their satirical pens to geography and general knowledge with equal mastery.

HORSE NONSENSE

Messrs Sellar and Yeatman now turn their enquiring pens to the subject of horses—and the people who ride, hunt and punt on them. Non-riders will find *Horse Nonsense* indispensable to their understanding of the topic: and riders will discover a lot of astonishing things about the Noble Animal which may have heretofore escaped them.

Jilly Cooper

SUPER MEN AND SUPER WOMEN

Her brilliantly funny guide to the sexes

Whatever their grading, Super Man or Slob, Super Woman or Slut, Jilly submits them all to remorseless scrutiny. In public and private, home, office or bed, none escapes her beady eye—from guardsmen to gigolos, debs to divorcees, stockbrokers to sex fiends, tarts to Tory ladies.

Frank Muir & Denis Norden

THE 'MY WORD!' STORIES

Probably the most popular radio programme in the world, 'My Word!' has countless fans in more than thirty-five countries. Its highlights are the outrageously funny spoof explanations of well-known sayings concocted by Frank Muir and Denis Norden, which have had listeners roaring with laughter for twenty years. Here is a collection of the best of their tall stories.

'a feast of fun from two very funny persons'
—Evening News

thelwell.

THREE SHEETS IN THE WIND

Arriving on a summer week-end at any stretch of water without one's own craft behind the car or swaying proudly at its moorings is like attending a dance with a broken leg—not to mention the damage to one's social status. Unable to bear being a second-class citizen any longer, Thelwell purchased his own boat and launched himself into unknown waters. But he found that learning to sail can be hazardous, and learning to speak a whole new technical language can be, to say the least, traumatic. So, ever mindful of the need to help his fellow men, he has produced this indispensable manual of instruction for sailors everywhere.

TOP DOG

As every experienced dog-owner knows, man's best friend is a complex bundle of appetites, instincts and winsome wiles. Few first-time pet-owners will realise, however, just what a responsibility they are taking on. So Thelwell has kindly provided them with this invaluable handbook full of advice on choosing, training, feeding, exercising and caring for our four-legged friends. It also emphasises the importance of protecting one's own interests—not to mention those of one's neighbours—for an ill-trained hound will soon develop a healthy disrespect for law and order. Here is a superb collection designed to give every dog-owner a new leash on life in the canine world.

thelwell.

UP THE GARDEN PATH
Thelwell's Guide to Gardening

It is well-known fact that you cannot make a beautiful garden by sitting with your feet up in the gazebo. With this in mind, and in an effort to bring relief to fellow sufferers, Thelwell has distilled all the necessary information in one convenient volume.

Up the Garden Path covers all aspects of gardening, from how to make a hole in the frozen fish pond to how to get your mower out of the shed, and includes an indispensable calendar of essential work throughout the year. Each piece of information is concise and pointed and is illustrated in a manner which makes its meaning crystal clear.

Here, then, is a gardener's handbook in the true sense of the word, designed to be held in one hand while the flame gun is kept going with the other.

THELWELL'S COMPLEAT TANGLER
Being a Pictorial Discourse of Anglers and Angling

Why do more men go fishing every week-end in Britain than go to football matches or any other sport? What do they really get up to when they abandon a warm bed before the crack of dawn, stuff a haversack with tins of assorted maggots, half a hundredweight of pulped bread and a folding campstool, and disappear into the drizzle?

It is estimated that well over one and a half million wives wish they knew the answer. It was clearly time that some sort of enquiry was made into the strange rituals of the cult, and its secrets exposed to the public gaze. After years of crawling through wet grass and conducting lonely vigils in distant torrents, Thelwell has at last presented his report.

thelwell.

A LEG AT EACH CORNER

Thelwell's Complete Guide to Equitation

After years of careful study from a safe distance,
Thelwell has prepared a unique and comprehensive
volume for the guidance of ambitious young
equestrians. *A Leg at Each Corner* covers the whole
field of equitation from how to get a pony to how to
prevent one from getting you; from how to pull his
tail to how to bandage your legs.

Books for horse lovers have been written before
but most suffer from a serious defect—they are
difficult to read on horseback. Not so this book.
Thelwell's information is short and to the point
and each item is illustrated with deadly clarity. It
is designed to be referred to in any emergency—at
the walk, trot or canter, or from the depths of a
blackthorn hedge.

THELWELL'S RIDING ACADEMY

Why is riding so popular? Why do our children
take to the saddle like the hordes of Ghengis
Khan? The answer is simple. The horse is the
transport of the future. In a few short years from
now when the last spaces on the road are plugged,
the internal combustion engine will be as obsolete
as the hot air balloon. When that day comes, woe to
those who have not learned how to get into a
saddle. And studied the art of staying there.

In other books, Thelwell has done much to
prepare us for future developments, but the
demand for more and yet more knowledge on the
subject is deafening.

*Angels on Horseback, Thelwell Country, A Leg at
Each Corner* and *Thelwell's Riding Academy* are
available as a boxed set in *Thelwell's Horse Box.*

thelwell.

and don't miss—

ANGELS ON HORSEBACK
—and elsewhere

PENELOPE

THELWELL COUNTRY

THELWELL'S BOOK OF LEISURE

THIS DESIRABLE PLOT
A Dream-House Hunter's Nightmare

Top humour from Magnum Books

These and other Magnum Books are available at your bookshop or newsagent. In case of difficulty orders may be sent to:—

Magnum Books,
Cash Sales Department,
P.O. Box 11,
Falmouth,
Cornwall, TR10 10QEN

Please send cheque or postal order, no currency, for purchase price quoted and allow the following for postage and packing:—

UK: 19p for the first book plus 9p per copy for each additional book up to a maximum of 73p.

BFPO & Eire: 19p for the first book plus 9p per copy for the next six books. Other Overseas Customers: 20p for the first book plus 10p per copy for each additional book.

While every effort is made to keep prices low, it is sometimes necessary to increase the prices at short notice. Magnum Books reserve the right to show new retail prices on covers which may differ from those previously advertised in the text or elsewhere.